Shaquille O'Neal: The Inspiring Story of One of Basketball's Greatest Centers

An Unauthorized Biography

By: Clayton Geoffreys

Table of Contents

Foreword

Every decade, there are a handful of players who come define their basketball generation. It is no surprise that Shaquille O'Neal, often known as simply Shaq, was one of those generational talents for those who watched basketball through the nineties and into the new millennium. Shaq brought a unique dominance to the center position that had not been seen in years. A four-time NBA champion and three-time NBA Finals MVP, Shaq was one of the best of his time. There is no doubt in reflecting back on his career that he lived up to being the first overall pick in the 1992 NBA Draft. He was such an influential player that he had his jersey retired by two different franchises: the Los Angeles Lakers and the Miami Heat. After retiring in 2011, Shaq shifted focus to grow his business ventures while remaining highly connected to the game as a TNT analyst. Thank you for purchasing *Shaquille O'Neal: The Inspiring Story of One of Basketball's Greatest Centers*. In this unauthorized biography, we will learn Shaquille O'Neal's incredible life story and impact on the game of basketball. Hope you enjoy and if you do, please do not forget to leave a review!

Also, check out my website at claytongeoffreys.com to join my exclusive list where I let you know about my latest books. To thank you for your purchase, you can go to my site to download a free copy of *33 Life Lessons: Success Principles, Career Advice & Habits of Successful People*. In the book, you'll learn from some of the greatest

1

thought leaders of different industries on what it takes to become successful and how to live a great life.

Cheers,

Clayton Geoffreys

Visit me at www.claytongeoffreys.com

Introduction

The NBA has had its share of dominant players that could lord over defenders and push around grown men inside the paint with ease. As they say, the NBA is a big man's league, and some of the best players the league has ever seen were among the greatest and most dominant men to have ever set foot on a hard wood floor. And wherever those dominant players went, success would usually follow.

One of the NBA's pioneering dominant players was George Mikan, who played for what was then the Minneapolis Lakers back in the 50's. At 6'10" and 250 pounds, Mikan would not be considered one of the biggest players in today's era. But back then, he was already among the largest in the league. Nobody could stop him in the paint on his way to five NBA titles.

The first truly dominant player in league history was Wilt Chamberlain. Standing above seven feet tall and weighing nearly 300 pounds of lean muscle mass, "Wilt the Stilt" used his height and strength advantage to bully players down under the basket. Chamberlain was rumored to be so strong that he could easily lift a man over 200 pounds using only one arm. He even once dunked the ball so hard that it broke an opposing player's toe. All of this strength and size were vital for Wilt Chamberlain to score 100 points in a single game. He even averaged over 50 points a game during one season while holding five of the top ten scoring averages in a single season. He was a man among boys back in the 60's era. Wilt would end up with two NBA titles, which he won during the twilight years of his career.

During the 80's and 90's, Karl Malone would use his bodybuilder strength and muscle to push opposing power forwards around when he bulled his way to easy baskets inside the paint. Because of how well-conditioned and dominant of a player Malone was, he was able to stay active until the age of 40. Eventually, Malone finished second in most points ever scored in a career. Sadly, Malone was always the bridesmaid to Michael Jordan's bride as he would never win an NBA championship during his era.

Later on, the likes of Yao Ming, who stood 7'6" and weighed over 300 pounds, was so tall and massive that it was nearly impossible to stop him especially because he was so mobile and skilled at his size. Nobody was able to contain Yao Ming, and it took repeated injuries for the giant man to finally go down and call it a career after capturing the imagination of a worldwide basketball audience.

As dominant and significant as those players mentioned above are, they all pale in comparison to the size of one of the NBA's biggest players concerning size and personality. No other NBA player in league history was as dominant inside the court while staying a dominant personality outside the hard floor as Shaquille O'Neal was.

Standing 7'1" and weighing over 330 pounds (some would even say he weighed close to 380 at one point), Shaquille O'Neal was tall and hulking for a basketball player. He was seven feet tall of pure mass, and nobody in the paint could take his beating once he decided to pound his way to the basket. And despite his sheer size, O'Neal was one of the most mobile and athletic big men in the league. During his early days, he would run the floor hard for fast break opportunities so quickly that not even guards could keep up with him. And when he was anywhere near the basket, his combination of leaping ability and mass was what he needed to dunk over the heads of opposing centers.

Despite his size and athletic ability, Shaquille O'Neal, or simply Shaq, was never all about using his massive frame to get baskets. Even if he was not as big as he was, O'Neal had enough skills and craftiness down at the low post to score points in the rarest of cases when equally big players were big and strong enough to hold their ground against his hulking frame. As an offensive weapon, Shaquille O'Neal was good and dominant enough that he would lead the league in points twice.

As the cornerstone of two franchises, Shaquille O'Neal never failed to deliver. With his size and dominance, he was always the first option on offense, especially when he could easily bull his way against much smaller defenders. For four years on his first team, the Orlando Magic, O'Neal showed the kind of size and athletic dominance that only Wilt Chamberlain has ever been able to display on the floor. He was a two-way threat that could block shots on the defense while sprinting down the court fast enough to finish transition plays. O'Neal would almost single-handedly piggyback the entire Orlando Magic franchise to the 1995 NBA Finals where they were swept by the Houston Rockets.

When Shaquille O'Neal moved over to Los Angeles to play for the Lakers and join the likes of Mikan, Chamberlain, and Abdul-Jabbar as one of the franchise's all-time greatest centers, he was immediately called upon to lead the team back to its former glory. Together with a young Kobe Bryant, Shaquille O'Neal would bring the Lakers to three consecutive NBA titles from 2000 to 2002. He would later win another title in 2006 when he was a member of the Miami Heat.

It was also the glitz and glamor of being in Los Angeles that catapulted Shaquille O'Neal from being a basketball superstar to a worldwide megastar. Appearing in movies, television shows, talks shows, and reality shows, Shaquille O'Neal became a global household name that was not only the biggest thing on the basketball court but was also the biggest megastar of his time during his peak years. His humor, love for life, jovial nature, and jolly giant attitude were what made him a charismatic figure everywhere he went.

While he would spend the final years of his NBA career as a journeyman for teams that needed his size and bright smile, Shaquille O'Neal's nearly two-decade dominance on the hardwood floor was only matched by his dominance as easily the most identifiable basketball star since Michael Jordan. He was recognizable not just because of his sheer size, but because of the comedic side that he brought to the game of basketball.

After retirement, Shaquille O'Neal never fully left basketball. He started working with the *TNT* broadcast crew for the NBA to deliver his analysis of today's modern era while also bringing with him his penchant for making the game lighter and funnier via segments such as *Shaqtin' a Fool* and his constant humorous jokes on *Inside the NBA*.

Known for names such as "The Diesel," "The Big Aristotle," "Superman," "Shaq Daddy," and other monikers that he goes by, Shaquille O'Neal would not only be known because of how he was the single biggest thing that has ever stepped foot inside the paint. It was also because of how he has always been larger than life itself. There is no wonder why Shaq is in the basketball Hall of Fame.

Chapter 1: Childhood and Early Life

The giant that would soon become Shaq was born on March 6, 1972, in Newark, New Jersey. Shaquille O'Neal was born to parents Lucille O'Neal and Joe Toney. Toney himself used to be one of the best guards in New Jersey when he was still in his prime. However, nothing more is shared between Shaq and Toney other than the latter's genetics and his aptitude for the game of basketball. Of course, Toney also claims that he was the one who gave Shaq his name. The young O'Neal was born Shaquille Rashaan, which Toney said meant "little warrior."[i] However, nothing about Shaq was small when it was all said and done.

Shaquille O'Neal and Joe Toney never met personally when the future megastar was still young. Toney was a hustler and had problems with drug addiction. He was in and out of jail because of his addiction to drugs and petty crimes such as stealing credit cards and forging checks. At that time, he never had the time or willingness to become a father because of the life of crime he lived.[i]

When Joe Toney was finally out of jail, it was too late for him to be a part of the young Shaquille O'Neal's life. Lucille had married Phillip Harrison who, like Toney, used to be a basketball player in the state of New Jersey back in the day. Harrison would enlist in the army and would quickly be promoted to sergeant. He would bring Lucille and the young boy he would raise as his own to Germany for a while.[i]

The first time that Shaq met Toney was when the former was ten years old, and the latter had just gotten out of prison for a three-year sentence. At that time, Shaq was already overgrown for his age at 6'4".[ii] He was wearing sneakers bigger than what most adults wore. But as Toney would describe his son back then, Shaq was a quiet wet-eyed boy that seemed nothing like the jolly giant of a man he is today. It would take several more years until father and son would meet again. As they parted, both O'Neal and Toney became very different people.[i]

Before Shaq would spend time with his new father, he would find that life in Newark was not easy. Drug dealers were out and about the neighborhood and even around their apartment. Luckily for O'Neal, his family was overprotective of him. His aunt Viv would try to scare away the dealers and bad influences, claiming that her nephew was too special of a child to be around their likes. She already saw the makings of a future basketball star in Shaquille O'Neal.[iii]

Other than his aunt Viv, Shaq spent his childhood days with his grandmother Odessa. O'Neal claims that his grandma was the perfect Christian woman and an avid churchgoer who never let the Bible out of her sight. For Shaq, she was a model of an exemplary woman and the person who told him never to stop dreaming big. He always felt safe around grandma Odessa as she kept a close watch on him, just as she did with her Bible.[iii]

Growing up was not so easy for Shaquille O'Neal. He knew he was a big boy. He was quickly outgrowing his shoes and his shirts. That was a big problem for his family, who he thought was poor that time. To make matters worse, he was called "freak" or "big foot" by neighborhood kids because of how big he was. Lucille, who was 6'2", knew the struggle of being tall. She even had to bring around Shaq's birth certificate all the time to show the bus driver and the fast-food counter that her son was still a child.[iii]

As Shaquille O'Neal would grow up with his new father Phillip Harrison, he would find himself moving from one military base to another before the family would finally settle in San Antonio, Texas, when Shaq was in high school. But before that, they spent more time in Newark than they did in Germany. Being a military father, Harrison was stern and strict though he treated Shaq as his flesh and blood. He would go as far as beating the young boy with his bare fists if he needed to.

Shaquille would try his hand at breakdancing when he was a young boy to distract people from noticing how big he was. He was good at it and was getting praises for being a good dancer. However, he would feel pain in his knees from time to time. Doctors would say he had a disease that was a result of how quickly he was growing. When he told his father, he got punched for getting sore knees as a result of all the dancing he was doing.

Dancing was not the only thing that made Shaq more comfortable with his size as a young boy. He started to act like "The Man" in school by being a big goofball and acting like a bully whenever he needed to. That did not sit well with Harrison, who would beat the child until he would learn that goofing around in class was not how he would get out of the life of poverty he was living.[iii]

The worst beatings came when Shaquille O'Neal was acting like a young thug in school. Being the goofball that he was, Shaq would often make fun of things in school to a fault. Kids would rat him out to the teacher. In turn, Shaq would beat them to a pulp. Of course, a worse beating waited for O'Neal back at home because Harrison simply did not want his son to end up like Toney.

Before Shaquille O'Neal reached his high school life, there were episodes where it would seem like he was following the footsteps of his father. Shaquille was young and adventurous to a fault. He once stole a car with his friends while the family was still stationed in Germany. When Harrison found out, he beat the young boy so hard that Shaquille O'Neal himself would call it the worst beating he has ever had as a child. Harrison, or "Sarge" as Shaq would like to call him, even once beat the young boy hard in a school restroom after a parent-teacher conference.[ii]

For Phillip Harrison, he never thought that the way he disciplined his adopted son was wrong. He never wanted Shaq to follow the footsteps of Toney. Harrison would rather pummel O'Neal until the young boy got the message rather than let him run loose in the streets where criminals and gangs would kill him and make him just another statistic in the crime-ridden streets of Newark. And for Shaquille O'Neal, he never once thought that it was child abuse. He understood that it was all about discipline and that he would never have been where he is right now if Sarge did not pummel the message into his head.[ii]

Nevertheless, Harrison still treated Shaquille as a son when the latter was not being a head case. Sarge taught O'Neal all the basics of basketball when the boy was still very young. But similar to how they do it in the jungle, Harrison would leave O'Neal alone when he was out there in the park playing against older and bigger men. He rarely accompanied Shaq to ballparks. He wanted the boy to learn on his own and become his own man. And when he saw that bigger, older players were pounding and bullying the young boy, Sarge never once stepped in to help his son. For him, it was up to Shaquille O'Neal himself to become a better player.[iii]

But sometimes Harrison would act like a tough coach on Shaquille O'Neal while teaching him the basics of being a center like Wilt Chamberlain, Bill Russell, and Kareem Abdul-Jabbar. Knowing how much bigger Shaq was than kids of his age, he would scold the young O'Neal whenever he would try to finesse his way for a bucket. Instead, Sarge would urge Shaquille to go at his defender's chest and score over him.[ii] That was one of the earliest accounts of how Shaquille O'Neal started to become a dominant force in the paint.

The 10-year-old Shaquille O'Neal was so good or dominant at that time that he was scoring 30 to 40 points over smaller youth teams while demolishing them with his post moves and hook shots without ever forgetting to involve his teammates by throwing outlet passes that Harrison, a guard, taught him to do. Sarge would remember how a father of another boy that Shaq just annihilated would claim that the young O'Neal was not 10. Shaquille O'Neal was just simply that good and dominant that Phillip Harrison claimed then and there that he would become the best big man in the world.[ii] He was not wrong with that claim. And before long, the world of preparatory basketball would come to see the next big legendary center.

Chapter 2: High School Career

While it was easy for Shaquille O'Neal to bully smaller defenders in the paint before he went to high school, things would not go as easy for him when he started playing against kids his age and size. He would go on to try out for his high school basketball team in his freshman year when he was still in Germany. At that time, Shaq believed he was about 6'8" and still very much growing.[iii]

Though Shaquille O'Neal was a large teenager back then, he believed he was awkward. He was still getting used to his massive body. He could not jump that well, nor could he dunk despite his height. The only thing going for him was that he had good footwork and a few point guard skills he practiced when he tried to become Magic Johnson.[iii]

When Shaq tried out for the basketball team, he got matched up with an upperclassman named Dwayne Clark, who was about his size back then. As far as skill and athleticism would go, Clark was miles ahead of O'Neal. He could dunk the ball hard and do fadeaway moves that Shaq could only dream of. Clark abused Shaquille O'Neal by faking inside moves and waiting for the younger teenager to bite on them. None of the coaches even bothered asking O'Neal his name. He got cut.

Shaquille O'Neal went back home to tell his dad that he got cut. Naturally, Sarge got mad at Shaq and told him to go back to the gym to work harder on his game. It was then and there when O'Neal realized his mistake: he was lazy. Shaq always liked doing things his way. He did not use his size to his advantage. Rather than using his size, he wanted to be like Magic Johnson or even Michael Jordan. However, Shaq also realized that he was so lazy that he even wanted to quit basketball rather than trying out for the junior varsity team.

But Harrison never quit on the young teenager. Sarge would pit the 6'8" behemoth of a young kid against grown men in a base full of soldiers. Those were not ordinary grown men. They were soldiers trained to be tough and physical. That was how Sarge wanted his son to train as a basketball player. He allowed military men to abuse and push Shaquille O'Neal around knowing well enough that his son would come out stronger and tougher than he ever was.

Back in the army base, a certain Ford McMurtry, who was an assistant coach for the high school team that cut Shaq, approached the young O'Neal and asked him if he would join the military base team he was building. Ford became one of the first mentors that Shaq had outside of his father. He made O'Neal less clumsy and more refined inside the paint with his footwork.[iii]

Another mentor of Shaq was a guy named Pete Popovich. Pete wondered why Shaquille O'Neal did not dunk, though he had the height to do it. Shaq said that his knees often bothered him. Pete would then help O'Neal with his weightlifting workout and had him work on his legs more. As Shaq himself would say, the leg workouts improved his vertical leap from 18 inches to a whopping 42 inches.[iii]

The bumbling giant of a teenager has turned into a high-flying big man.

Shaquille O'Neal and his family would move back to the United States because his father was assigned to San Antonio. When the family arrived in Texas, Shaq started attending Robert G. Cole High School in 1987. At that time, he was an unknown. Nobody knew where he came from. All the known young talents had developed in the AAU, where Shaq never even played a single game in his life. And unfortunately for O'Neal, he could not join the team because his transfer was already too late.

Initially, Shaquille O'Neal wanted to join the football team while waiting for the next basketball season. However, Sarge would not allow it out of fear that O'Neal might get injured. After all, basketball was the only way Shaq could get out of poverty. Instead, O'Neal would take part as the football team's statistician. Despite not being on the team, he did the same drills as the guys on the team did.[iii] The football drills helped O'Neal become a more agile athlete.

Come his junior year, Shaquille O'Neal had grown to at least 6'10" already. In one of his first games, O'Neal remembered how his father had an impact on his attacking and dunking mentality as a baller. Back then, Shaq was too afraid of dunking the ball in fear that he might miss it. He had never dunked the ball in a game his entire life. At one point during the match, he had an open path to the basket. Instead of dunking it hard, he did a finger roll.

Sarge would pull Shaq out of the huddle during a timeout. He told O'Neal to stop emulating legends such as Julius Erving and George Gervin by doing a finger roll. Instead, he wanted his son to become his own man, to become Shaquille O'Neal. After the timeout, Shaq dunked the ball as hard as he could the next time he had a chance to do so. He realized that it was not difficult to slam the ball down like a monster. He also liked the terror in his defenders' eyes whenever he would dunk the ball on their heads.[iii]

While Shaquille O'Neal realized how unstoppable he was inside the paint when he was dunking the ball hard on defenders' heads, he also thought that he should not be a one-trick pony. Because of that, he decided to watch some of the game's best players and try to emulate their style and moves on the court as much as he could.

The first man he tried to emulate was Patrick Ewing, a center who played for the New York Knicks during those days. Ewing always seemed like he had a scowl on his face and it was as if he was trying to beat up everyone else on the court. O'Neal liked that. He wanted to strike fear into the hearts of his opponents. He would start to wear a scowl as if he was out there to draw blood.

Another guy he began to emulate was Rony Seikaly, who was still in college at that time but would soon play in the NBA and spend most of his years with the Miami Heat. Seikaly used to pull his legs up whenever he dunked the ball. Shaq loved that and took it as one of his signature moves. O'Neal also saw tapes of David Robinson, a military man that was the talk of the town in San Antonio at that time. Using his agility, Robinson always ran the floor hard. He also had a quick spin move that allowed him to blow past defenders at the post. O'Neal worked hard to copy those from Robinson.[iii]

With Shaquille O'Neal dominating the paint as Cole High School's biggest star, the Cougars were the best team in San Antonio. Shaq entirely changed the school's basketball team's culture. Cole High was a small school compared to the other programs in the region. Their budget was not as big as the others. The basketball team did not even have a locker room. But somehow, Shaq led them to an undefeated season during his junior year.

Shaquille O'Neal quickly became a celebrity of sorts in San Antonio basketball. Scouts and college coaches from all over the country would flock into Cole High School to watch O'Neal during practices. This went on until the Cole Cougars reached the state finals. In the state finals, Shaq and company faced Liberty Hill, a team full of shooters. But with a few ticks left on the clock and with the Cougars down by a few manageable points, O'Neal would miss two free throws to the demise of his team. For Shaq, that was when the free throw curse started.[iii]

Despite the loss, Shaquille O'Neal was still the hottest topic in high school basketball because of how he was so big and dominant at his age. Before his senior year got started, he went around the country visiting five potential college programs that wanted him. After all, he was the hottest high school prep prospect during that time.

The first school that Shaq visited was North Carolina, where Michael Jordan made a name for himself. However, Shaq thought that he was not the school's first choice as they were also shopping another seven footer. He then went to North Carolina State. He liked the program but thought that he wanted to be his star on his team. NC State already had the original "Shack," a guy named Charles Shackleford, starring for the team.

Shaquille O'Neal would consider going to Texas University. However, he thought that it was too close to home. O'Neal wanted to be free from his family after several years of Sarge's strict parenting. After that, Shaq went to Illinois but thought that the team was already too good for him. O'Neal always wanted to be the star on the team.

Finally, Shaquille O'Neal visited LSU. Dale Brown, who Shaq met back in Germany, was coaching the team. Other than his relationship with Brown, O'Neal wanted to go to LSU because he felt that he was wanted there. The coach wanted him. The players welcomed him. Even the entire school were chanting for him to come to LSU. Because of that, he decided to pack up for LSU after high school.[iii]

Back in Cole High School, Shaquille O'Neal would lead the Cougars to an undefeated season once again. O'Neal became the talk of the town not only because of how good he was but because of the news that he had decided to become a big name college player by going to

LSU. Games were sold out, and little children were asking for his autograph.

But when Shaquille O'Neal noticed how his head was getting too big and how his team was noticing that he was making everything about himself, the young giant humbled himself and got his teammates going by passing the ball more often instead of trying to get the attention of the scouts and media. But when he was needed to dominate during the regional finals, he made Liberty Hill pay in their rematch. Shaq finished the game with 44 points and 18 rebounds to give Cole High School the state championship berth.

In the state finals, the Cole Cougars went up against Clarksville. The problem for O'Neal in that game was that Clarksville had a center named Tyrone Washington who was shooting jumpers out on the perimeter over Shaq. Come the second half, O'Neal adjusted his game and dared Washington to shoot from the perimeter as he protected the paint. Shaq, who was also in foul trouble the entire game, was forced to show his array of jumpers from the perimeter so as to protect himself from the risks of an offensive foul.[iii] In the end, Cole would win the state title over Clarksville.

As the dust settled, the team celebrated their first state title win. It was all because of Shaquille O'Neal, and the entire world knew that to be a fact. Shaq would end the season with a state record of 791 rebounds in a single season. But no record was sweeter than winning the first major championship he had in his life. Shaq was not only a dominant force from then on. He also became a winner as he would soon pack his bags to head to Louisiana.

Chapter 3: College Career

Freshman Year

The moment Shaq entered LSU, he loved it and would even say that it was the best years of his life.[iii] The business major enjoyed every bit of his college living at the university. He had free food on the table, could work for some extra cash during his spare time, and was even studying on scholarship. On top of that, he loved playing for Dale Brown, a man he would call one of his best friends.

Coming into his freshman year at LSU, Shaquille O'Neal had a lot of expectations on his shoulders as he was asked to anchor the middle. However, the seven footer would have to contend with minutes against a fellow tall center. Stanley Roberts himself was a talented center. He was arguably more skillful than Shaq ever was. Roberts could shoot turnaround jumpers and could even extend his range all the way to the three-point line. He was an exceptional big man and was even probably better than Shaq was.

Unlike Shaq, Stanley Roberts was not a rookie. He was not allowed to play his freshman season because of academic problems. Because of that, he was not given the same rookie treatment as Shaq did. O'Neal would call Roberts a cool dude. He liked the guy because he was not a bad person in his estimation. The only thing bad about Roberts were his grades, but that was a different story.

Coming into the 1989-90 season, LSU had a pair of seven footers. One was the large and burly freshman named Shaquille O'Neal. The other was Stanley Roberts, who was probably the most skilled seven footer that time. However, the main man of the team was Chris Jackson, who would later be renamed to Mahmoud Abdul-Rauf. Jackson was as fine a guard as anyone else in the country. He led the nation in scoring the past season. He could shoot the ball from anywhere on the court. Because of his skills, LSU chose Jackson as their first option despite having a pair of seven footers that would often play together out on the floor.

Shaq's freshman year was a humbling experience. He always thought that he was the biggest star on the court when he was in high school. Little did he know that every other guy on the team had that exact mindset. Jackson was the team's star and, in O'Neal's words, was revered as a "basketball god" on campus. Roberts, on the other hand, was a skillful center he could not defend down in the paint though he could dominate him on the offensive end.

Shaquille O'Neal would not start his first four games. Dale Brown told him that he thought that the expectations might weigh down on the freshman's broad shoulders. But O'Neal always thought that it was because Stanley Roberts was better than he was. Roberts had it all. He had the skills, money, and popularity to boot his status as a college star. However, he was not the model athlete. Roberts had bad grades and would spend all night partying. Because of that, he would usually miss classes and would often pass on pickup games or even team practices. In Shaq's mind, Roberts would have been a good player had he worked on his game more and partied less.[iii]

Shaquille O'Neal would credit Stanley Roberts for making him who he was. He could not defend Roberts down at the post when they would play together. Because of that, he worked hard on his defense. On top of all that, Roberts was an avid drinker that had little to no time to play pickup basketball because he was always hung over. Shaq would see the effects of drinking too much alcohol because of Roberts. He would try to avoid drinking as much as possible during his time in LSU.

Shaquille O'Neal, ever the jovial gentle giant, had other ways of having fun. He spent time with a group of basketball friends that had the same sense of humor as he did. Of course, being the biggest of the bunch, O'Neal stood out. Shaq and his friends did funny antics on campus that got them the attention of the student population. They loved how humorous their freshman star was. Shaq was making friends every day because of who he was as a person. Despite all that, O'Neal still had to focus on his studies. He had the highest GPA in the team during his freshman year.

With Shaquille O'Neal on the team, the LSU Tigers were a fast-paced up-tempo team. They loved scoring the ball a lot, and Shaq was a part of that run-and-gun style of play because he ran the floor hard despite his size. But the problem for Shaq was also his size. He was so big and aggressive out on the court that he often struggled with foul trouble. He played only 28 minutes a game during his freshman year.

Knowing that his aggressive and physical nature would often get him in foul trouble, Shaq himself told Dale Brown how he wanted to focus more on defense and rebounding rather than scoring. O'Neal would do just that. He averaged a bit under 14 points a game and led the team in rebounding with 12 a night. One of his best games of the season was against Loyola Marymount in an overtime classic. Shaq had a triple-double of 20 points, 24 rebounds, and 12 blocks in that win. Throughout the season, he also averaged 3.6 blocks and had a total of 115. That was the first time someone in the Southeastern Conference went over a hundred blocks in a season.

The team's leading scorer was Chris Jackson who, despite being only 6'1", was averaging 27.8 points and was making nearly three three-pointers per game. He would be named the conference's Player of the Year. Meanwhile, the other seven footer, Stanley Roberts, managed to average 14 points and nearly ten rebounds despite being lazy and out of shape most of the season.

The LSU Tigers went into the NCAA Tournament with a 23-8 record and would beat Villanova in the first round. Georgia Tech was not an easy opponent in the second round. They had a bunch of shooters that spaced the floor well and could drain shots over defenders. With

O'Neal and Roberts, LSU were trading inside two-point dunks for the three-pointers that Georgia Tech's players were draining. As a result, the Tigers lost the game by three points in overtime.

At the end of the season, Chris Jackson would announce that he would leave the team and try his hand at the NBA Draft. He was chosen third overall by the Denver Nuggets and would have a respectable NBA career as one of the most underrated shooters the league has ever seen. But what Shaq remembered the most from him was how he would not share the ball during that loss to Georgia Tech. Nevertheless, O'Neal would call the little man one of the best shooters he has ever seen.

Meanwhile, Dale Brown handled the issue with Stanley Roberts. He told Roberts to move on to the NBA because he felt that he had done everything he could at LSU. But that was a nice way of putting it. Everybody knew how lazy Roberts was. He was blowing off classes, getting drunk all night, and hanging out with his girlfriend more rather than studying or even practicing. But Roberts would not leave because he felt like Brown only wanted Shaq to have more touches. He would spend the summer taking classes, but failures convinced him to go pro. He missed the NBA Draft and would instead spend a season in Spain as a professional basketball player. Stanley Roberts would make the NBA, but injuries and laziness got the better of him. With Chris Jackson and Stanley Roberts gone, Shaquille O'Neal would finally get his limelight as "The Man" in LSU.

Sophomore Season

Shaq's freshman year at LSU was already impressive on its own considering he averaged a double-double. He could even have gone pro had he decided to skip the remaining years of his college career. Had he decided so, he would have surely been a top five pick. However, Shaq wanted to develop more in college before trying his hand in the NBA.

Shaquille O'Neal was the identity of the LSU Tigers during his sophomore year. Chris Jackson was not there shooting nearly 30 shots a game. Stanley Roberts was not there anymore to share the paint with Shaq. All that was left was this seven footer that weighed about 300 pounds of pure mass. Shaq was both the offensive and defensive anchor of the team.

There was simply no stopping Shaquille O'Neal that season. He was a man mountain that clogged the paint on defense and one that dunked on defenders on the offensive end. This was the first time that the world got to see how truly dominant Shaq was against even the toughest college opponents. The big man averaged 27.6 points on nearly 63% shooting. He also added 14.7 rebounds and five huge blocks a night.

Not as good of a team as they were the last season, the LSU Tigers could not dominate the SEC. They would have won the SEC title had they beaten Mississippi State in the final game before the conference tournament. But Shaq had to sit that game out due to a leg injury because Dale Brown feared he might aggravate it. O'Neal would also sit out a game against Auburn State during the conference tournament because of the same injury. LSU lost that one as well.

LSU was still able to make the NCAA Tournament though the injured O'Neal could not play as well as he would have liked. He scored 27 points and 16 rebounds when the Tigers lost to UConn in the opening round. While O'Neal could not win a title that season, he did emerge as arguably college basketball's best player. He became the first player in SEC history to lead the conference in points, rebounding, blocks, and field goal percentage. On top of all that, Shaq was named the SEC and Associated Press Player of the Year.

After his sophomore year, Shaquille O'Neal would have already been ready to go to the NBA, where he would have arguably been the top pick of the draft. However, he felt that he was not yet ready, not only concerning his skills, but his education. Taking up Business Management in LSU, Shaq thought that he still needed to learn more about business because he knew that basketball was not going to be there for him forever. He felt like he needed more education.[iii]

Junior Year

Dale Brown already knew how dominant Shaq was going to be when he decided to go pro. However, he also knew that O'Neal was not going to rely on his raw power forever. He would bring in big names to LSU to help teach Shaquille O'Neal more fundamental skills.

Brown brought Kareem Abdul-Jabbar to teach the skyhook, Bill Walton for defensive fundamentals, and Olympic sprinter Carl Lewis to instill fundamentals of proper sprinting.[iii] All that would help O'Neal become an even more dominant monster inside the paint.

Shaquille O'Neal would remain his utterly dominant self the entire junior year of his college career. He averaged 24 points, 14 rebounds, and a nation-leading 5.3 blocks a night. He also shot 61.5% from the floor. Considering that he was not able to win the Naismith and Wooden awards in his sophomore year, he was aiming to win it that season.

However, O'Neal could not win those awards. Instead, the awards went to Duke's senior center Christian Laettner, who was averaging 21.5 points and eight rebounds. While Laettner's numbers may not be on par with Shaq's, he was as skilled of a center as one could ever be based on how O'Neal remembers his first encounter with him. Laettner was beating O'Neal using fundamental plays such as backdoor cuts and jumpers from the perimeter instead of simply banging bodies with the bigger man.

When Shaq and Laettner faced during the 1991-92 season, O'Neal dominated the skinnier center. O'Neal heard more of Laettner's name than he did his own. He wanted to be the more hyped center coming into the draft. He wanted to be number one. Because of that, Shaquille O'Neal came in dunking on his defender's head while registering 27 points and 12 rebounds. However, Duke would win that game to the dismay of O'Neal and LSU.

It was during Shaq's junior season when teams started to foul him hard and purposely send him to the line. In a game against Tennessee during the SEC Tournament, O'Neal got fouled so hard that he retaliated harder than he ever had since Dale Brown told him to hit back when he was getting hit unnecessarily. A melee broke out, and Shaq was suspended in their next game in the tournament. LSU lost that one.

Shaquille O'Neal and the LSU Tigers would also lose early in the second round of the NCAA Tournament. They could not beat Indiana. After that, whispers began to surface about O'Neal's ability to win and lead a team. But then again, he could not be blamed for the team's losses. After all, he did have 36 points, 12 rebounds, and five blocks in what was his final game in college.

Three months before the annual NBA Draft, Shaquille O'Neal declared himself eligible. There was nothing left to do at LSU. He had already learned what he needed to learn and developed the skills he could learn in college. It was time for him to go to the NBA. However, unlike his personality, O'Neal quietly left the school. There were no farewell tours or parties, nor was there a big announcement. It was time he parted with the school.

The Dream Team Snub

Before Shaq left college, he was part again of another snub. O'Neal had already been snubbed for the Naismith and Wooden awards when Laettner won them. But that was not the only time when Christian Laettner would be chosen ahead of him for what many believed would have been the highest honor in all of basketball.

Back in 1991, the United States had just decided to form the very first Olympic basketball team composed of NBA players when FIBA allowed announced back in 1989 that they were going to allow professional basketball players to compete in the Olympics. It was called the "Dream Team" because of the sheer talent the roster had. The team was headlined by household names such as Michael Jordan, Karl Malone, Magic Johnson, Larry Bird, Charles Barkley, and Patrick Ewing. They were flanked by equally legendary players such as Scottie Pippen, John Stockton, Chris Mullin, David Robinson, and Clyde Drexler. There were 12 allowable slots, but only 11 players came from the NBA. The last roster spot was reserved for a standout college player.

It would have been an honor for any college player to be named a member of what is still considered the greatest team ever assembled in the history of basketball. All of the names on that roster were worthy of the Hall of Fame. If they were to give the final roster spot to a college player, it had to be a player that would someday also become part of the Hall of Fame.

Similar to the Naismith and Wooden awards, the final roster spot came down to a choice between Shaquille O'Neal and Christian Laettner. But in the end, Laettner was given the spot on May 12, 1992. Laettner had one of the most storied college basketball careers in history. He was a back-to-back NCAA champion in 1991 and 1992. However, he was most remembered for the game-winning shot he made in a game against Kentucky to determine the final member of the Final Four in 1992. That game was considered the greatest college basketball game of all time.

As far as awards would go, Laettner was more decorated than O'Neal. He was the college player of the year in 1992, the Most Outstanding Player of the NCAA Tournament in 1991, a two-time national champion, and an All-American in 1992. He also holds numerous records in the NCAA Tournament and was a consistent contributor in Duke, a school known not only for its academic excellence, but also for being one of the best basketball programs in college. However, Laettner was not Shaquille O'Neal.

Shaq would later admit that he was upset that Laettner was chosen over him to become part of the greatest team ever assembled in basketball history.[iv] But he also realized how much better Laettner was a fit than he was to join that team. Though O'Neal was the bigger, stronger, and more explosive center of the two, Laettner was the more skilled and polished one. It was a common belief back then that, due to the differences in rules and styles between the NBA and international basketball, post-up centers could not do well in the

Olympics. With his perimeter jumpshot, Laettner was the better fit of the two, though it would have been fun to see O'Neal dunking hard on international players' heads.

Though Christian Laettner ended up with more championships and awards than Shaq did in college in addition to being a member of the Dream Team, he would not have the same kind of professional career that O'Neal would have in the NBA. Shaquille O'Neal would have been a better choice on that Dream Team as far as talent and superstar power were concerned. Nevertheless, Laettner would also become a Hall of Fame inductee similar to his fellow Dream Team teammates for what he accomplished as a college basketball player rather than for what his NBA career turned out to be. As for O'Neal, his superstar run would not end in college, unlike Laettner. He was still going to dominate on the NBA stage.

Chapter 4: NBA Career

Getting Drafted

The 1992 NBA Draft was not the most star-studded class. However, the consensus top three picks, who were all centers, were the cream of the crop and were already considered ready to be big-time players in the NBA. Included in those three players were Georgetown center Alonzo Mourning and Duke big man Christian Laettner. But among the consensus top three picks, one man stood out. Everybody wanted to Shaquille O'Neal on their team. Because of that, the annual draft lottery unofficially became the Shaq Sweepstakes. Whichever team was lucky enough to draw the first overall pick might as well have won a hundred million dollars because that was what Shaquille O'Neal was worth, and it was for a good reason.

The first thing anybody in the world would notice about Shaquille O'Neal was his sheer size. Back then, the 20-year-old young man was already bigger than almost any other player in the NBA. He stood up with a towering 7'1" frame. He was as tall as David Robinson. Shaq also had long arms that measured 7'7". But what set him apart from all other centers that had a similar height and wingspan was his body.

Saying that Shaquille O'Neal had an NBA-ready body was an understatement. The big young man weighed in at about 294 pounds in his junior year at LSU. Coming into the NBA Draft, he was nearing 300 pounds. What was surprising about his size was that he was a young man of pure lean muscle mass back then. He was so big, heavy, and strong that he was practically the center of gravity inside the paint. There was no way any other big man could push him out of the paint. And using his sheer size and weight, Shaq was bullying the opposition under the basket.

There have been a lot of tall and massive players in the history of the NBA. As far as size was concerned, Shaquille O'Neal was not a rarity. But size was not the only thing that made O'Neal such a physical specimen. He was freakishly athletic. During pre-draft measurements, he had a vertical leap of 36 inches. He once claimed that he could even jump higher than 40 inches off the ground when he was younger.[iii] On top of that, he could run the floor like a freight train on the loose. O'Neal was not your typical slow-footed bumbling giant. He was an athlete that sprinted the length of the court instead of jogging slowly while guards had already crossed the half court line five seconds ago. For a man as big as he was, his vertical leap and ability to sprint were what made him an athletic freak of nature.

Shaq's size and strength were where every major part of his game started. As urged by his father, Shaquille O'Neal used his physical tools to bully defenders in the paint. Sarge did not want him to finesse his way for two points. He wanted Shaq to run straight at his defender and dunk the ball down on his head. That was how O'Neal scored most of his points. He used his size and strength to get a good position inside the paint. And when the ball came to him, it would take only one power dribble or a single turn from his massive shoulders for him to get up a good shot under the basket.

But using his strength to bully defenders by aggressively backing down on them was not the only way that Shaq could score inside the paint. O'Neal has good footwork at the low post. He used his footwork to pull off post spin moves whenever he did not get the ball at a deep spot in the paint. And with Shaq's massive shoulders, it was difficult for any player to defend his spin move down at the block. Shaquille O'Neal also had a nifty skyhook that he learned from watching Kareem Abdul-Jabbar and by learning from the man himself when the legendary center once visited him in LSU.

While O'Neal could do spin moves and hook shots from the low post, arguably his deadliest move was the drop step. When he got the ball in a good position near the basket, and when he got his defender sealed behind him, O'Neal stepped a foot behind his opponent and would do a single turn of his shoulder to the baseline along with one dribble to get behind his man. With that move, he had an open look near or under the basket while his defender was helpless to stop him.

Once he did a drop step, there was no stopping him one-on-one. Shaq's large frame helped him carve enough space with the drop step to the point that defenders would have trouble recovering in time before he could even dunk the ball down or get a simple finish under the basket. The only thing stopping Shaq when he did that move was to make sure a help defender was already there before he turned his shoulder. But that never stopped Shaq from bulldozing the help defender as well.

Shaq would even do a modified version of the drop step that he did with contact. When he gets the ball down low, O'Neal muscles his way against a defender with a single dribble. With that initial contact, Shaq gets his defender off balanced enough that he could turn his shoulder to the basket undeterred for an easy slam or lay in. That was a move he often did to get taller centers too off balanced that they could neither jump up to block the shot nor recover in time to bother him.

For a man of his size, O'Neal was not merely a half court post player. Playing in the fast-paced style of the LSU Tigers especially during his freshman year, Shaq was used to running the length of the floor like a freight train that would sometimes even outrun opposing guards. No other center in college could match O'Neal's foot speed. He could sprint the floor like a charging rhino. That made him an easy target for passes during transition opportunities. And when the floor was clear, he would even sometimes bring the ball down himself using handles he developed while trying to emulate Magic Johnson back when he was young. Shaquille O'Neal could go coast to coast from a rebound all the way to an athletic play on the other end of the floor.

Defensively, Shaquille O'Neal was always a beast down in the paint. He was an intimidating shot-blocking presence that no slasher would ever dare challenge. He was not merely big, tall, and long when defending the basket. He was also athletic enough to get up high to swat away shots all the way to the bleachers. And when he was not blocking shots, his large presence alone inside the paint was enough to deter players from venturing down low. O'Neal's wide frame also made it difficult for players to get around him. No other center would dare try to push him at the low post or even try to pull a spin on him because he was so big and broad in the paint.

Rebounding was an obvious part of the package for Shaquille O'Neal. While some centers his size would have trouble rebounding the ball because of their mobility limitations and inability to go vertical, Shaq was a different breed of athlete. With his size, he boxes out opposing rebounders or gets inside rebounding position with ease. And using his athletic abilities, O'Neal gets up high to collar the offensive or defensive rebound while opposing rebounders stand helpless to stop him or put a body on him.

Though Shaquille O'Neal was a once-in-a-lifetime prospect that could inevitably turn a franchise around 360 degrees, the big man did have some chinks in his armor. Offensively, Shaquille O'Neal may be unstoppable inside the paint, especially with his size, strength, athleticism, and footwork. However, he was an unpolished big man that did not have the touch from anywhere farther than 10 feet away from the basket. O'Neal could hardly hit a jump shot to save his life. He claimed to have a jumper early on in his basketball years. However, that was a part of his game that was left undeveloped when he reached college.

Free throws were also a primary issue in his game. O'Neal was so big and unstoppable under the basket that the only way to slow him down was to foul him. From the 15-foot line, he was an awful shooter. He shot barely 60% from the free throw line in his three years in LSU. This led to teams often fouling him on purpose to save themselves from the easy points that Shaq would have put up on the board with a dunk or open lay in. Teams would rather gamble on his free throw shooting than getting him going with dunks.

Defensively, O'Neal was a beast inside the paint with all the blocks he got and by becoming an intimidating presence. However, Shaq's mobility was often hindered by his size. He may have been a good sprinter on the dead run, but his lateral movement was just the same as any other player standing over seven feet. On pick and roll situations, he struggled to defend perimeter players when he switched out. And even when defending centers, Shaq struggled defending against those that could hit perimeter jumpers because he was too slow to cover them outside the paint.

But even with his limitations, there was no arguing that Shaquille O'Neal was the top prospect in the 1992 NBA Draft. He was so valued that the 11 teams that vied for the top pick of the draft lottery all had customized O'Neal jerseys from their teams. The 1992 NBA Draft might have well been called the Shaq Draft because all the teams wanted him on board. But to the dismay of 10 other franchises, the Orlando Magic won the top overall pick.

There was no questioning who the Orlando Magic were going to choose. They were going to take Shaquille O'Neal no matter what. But the problem was whether Shaq wanted to play for them. Initially, what O'Neal wanted was to play with a team with good weather. He did not want to play for a cold climate city and preferred warmer ones.[iii] This made Orlando an ideal spot for him to play.

But Shaquille O'Neal held off trying to meet the Orlando Magic ownership and executives. It was only two days before the actual draft itself when Shaq went to Orlando to meet the front office and owners. O'Neal was given a tour of what was to become his next destination even before he was drafted. He was out there with his family. He liked the team owners and the city. Orlando, in turn, adored him back.

When the draft night was nearing, Shaquille O'Neal even had doubts that he was the rightful consensus top overall pick. For a man that had so much confidence in his skills and capabilities, he was still questioning whether he deserved to be the star of the draft class. The man that was on the mind of Shaq was none other than Christian Laettner. Laettner had tools that O'Neal did not have. He could hit the jumper, had better footwork, was mentally matured, and was the more accomplished college player. But to everyone else's mind, there was no doubt who was going first. Shaq had no reasons to doubt himself.

On draft night, the obvious came true. The Orlando Magic chose Shaquille O'Neal with their number one overall draft pick. Team ownership made it feel like Shaq was wanted. They organized a viewing party at Orlando's arena. About ten thousand people watched and cheered on Shaq as he was going up on stage to wear the Magic hat. For Shaq, it was the same feeling he had when LSU cheered for him when they heard he was coming over to Baton Rouge.[iii]

But the Orlando Magic were nearly not able to draft Shaquille O'Neal. Back then, the draft was held in Portland, Oregon because of the FIBA Americas tournament held there. When it was time for the Magic to pick their rookie, they had five minutes to do so. Of course, they did not need five minutes to say they wanted Shaq to come to Orlando. But technical difficulties nearly hindered the front office from transmitting their choice to the Orlando Magic representative in Portland. It would take a direct phone call to the NBA's New York office for the Magic to relay to the agent in Portland that they were choosing Shaquille O'Neal with only seconds to spare.[v] Had they missed out on that opportunity, O'Neal would have went to Charlotte instead.

As the draft proceeded, the Charlotte Hornets selected Alonzo Mourning with their second overall pick. Then, Christian Laettner was selected third by the Minnesota Timberwolves. Anybody else that went after those three players went unnoticed because only the top three picks were thought of as the ones that had star potential. Only five players in that class of 1992 would become All-Stars. The first three were the previously mentioned top three picks. Another future All-Star was Tom Gugliotta, who was chosen sixth overall, while the other one was late first round draftee Latrell Sprewell. But among all those five future stars, no one was literally or figuratively bigger than Shaquille O'Neal. Alone, he was far more valuable than those four other players. That was how much of a franchise changer Shaq was as he was coming into his rookie year with the Orlando Magic.

Rookie Season

Coming into his rookie season in Orlando, Shaquille O'Neal was immediately the face of an expanding franchise looking to get some credibility in a league ran by stars. The team was perfect for Shaq. He did not have to share the paint with another seven footer. It was a team full of young shooters like Nick Anderson and Dennis Scott. They also had veteran playmaker Scott Skiles, whose mentality was always to pass the ball first. Shaq was in the best situation he could ever be in Orlando because he was instantly The Man.

But O'Neal came into the NBA with serious competition at his position. That era of the NBA was the "Golden Age" of centers. The league was enjoying how much centers dominated the league, though most of the attention went to guys such as Jordan and Barkley. The Houston Rockets had Hakeem Olajuwon, who was considered the best at his position back then. The San Antonio Spurs, who Shaq watched back in high school, had David Robinson manning the middle. The New York Knicks was headlined by Patrick Ewing.

Shaquille O'Neal's first ever official NBA game was on November 6, 1992, against the Miami Heat. It was not the best game for Shaquille O'Neal. He struggled to adjust to the differences between college physicality and that of the NBA. He was mostly in and out of the game because of foul trouble. Nevertheless, he made the plays that mattered. He made half of his eight baskets to score a total of 12 points. He also ended up grabbing 18 monster rebounds and blocking three blocks in only 32 minutes of play. He would foul out of the game, but the Magic would win by 10 points.

One night later, Shaquille O'Neal would lead the Orlando Magic to a 2-0 start to the season when they faced the Washington Bullets (now Wizards). O'Neal managed to stay long in the game that night. He played 40 minutes, though he also almost fouled out. It was another big double-double game for Shaq, who had already dubbed himself "Superman" at that early point in his career. Superman finished the game with 22 points, 15 rebounds, and four blocks.

After a setback against the Hornets, Shaquille O'Neal would have his first truly dominant game in the NBA. In a 27-point win against the Bullets on November 12, Shaq made 12 of his 19 shots while finishing the game with his first ever 30-20 outing. He had 31 points, 21 rebounds (with nine coming from the offensive end), and four blocks. O'Neal would then finish the next three games scoring 29 points and blocking three blocks in all of them while averaging 16.7 rebounds. The Magic won two of those three outings.

In O'Neal's first seven games of the season, there was simply no stopping the young man. Shaq was averaging 26.7 points, 16.7 rebounds, and 3.3 blocks at that point of the season. He was shooting nearly 58% from the floor. There was no game where he shot less than 50% from the floor as he was yet to face a top caliber center early on in his rookie season. And with him leading the way, the Magic would only lose two of their first seven games.

But coming into his eighth game of the season, Shaquille O'Neal would finally get to face one of the most elite centers in the league. That night of November 21 was the first time he would ever go head to head with the New York Knicks' Patrick Ewing in a road trip game in the Big Apple. Before the match started, Shaq met Ewing for the first time in his career. He came up to the big man he used to idolize back when he was in college and tried to get a handshake. Ewing, ever the competitive big man, declined the handshake and instead told the 20-year-old mammoth of a young man that he would "bust him up" in the game.[iv]

For O'Neal, he thought that Ewing and every other center out there in the league were aching to get a piece of him, and they had a good reason to do so. Shaquille O'Neal, as a rookie, was getting more attention than any other player in the entire NBA aside from Michael Jordan.[iv] It was rightfully so because he was putting up monster numbers and was living up to the hype as the NBA's next big thing. But then Ewing ended up making things tough for him that game.

For the first time in his NBA career, O'Neal could not dominate an opposing center. It was not because Patrick Ewing was bigger than him. Shaq was a lot bigger, but Ewing had the experience. He ended up limiting O'Neal to a miserable 39% shooting night. That was the first time Shaq shot below 50% in his NBA career. Shaquille O'Neal finished that game with 18 points, 17 rebounds, and three blocks. Meanwhile, Ewing would get the win along with 15 points and nine rebounds. He did not have the best night of his life, but he limited Shaq's offense.

Things only got tougher for Shaquille O'Neal. In his next game four days after banging with Patrick Ewing down in the paint, Superman would get to go head-to-head with the Houston Rockets' Hakeem Olajuwon for the first time. Olajuwon himself was big and athletic. However, his size and athleticism were not his best weapons. The Rockets center arguably had the best footwork among any big man in the history of the NBA. He used his superior skill down at the low post to get defenders off-balance with fakes, spins, and counter-moves that nobody in the history of the NBA has been able to stop. On top of all that, Olajuwon was just as dominant on the defensive end and would eventually end up as the NBA's all-time shot blocker.

Shaq would find out how difficult of a cover and how great of a defender Olajuwon was. While Shaq had a good shooting night in that game, Hakeem was making it tough for him to get shots or even get the ball at a good position. Shaq would only put up 12 shots in that game and finished with 12 points and 13 rebounds. Olajuwon had 22 points, 13 rebounds, and five blocks. O'Neal would later admit that Hakeem Olajuwon was the only center he could not solve and intimidate on both ends of the floor.[vi] Orlando did come out of that game with a win despite a subpar performance from their star rookie.

Bouncing back, Shaquille O'Neal would have 22 points, 20 rebounds, and seven blocks in the middle of a four-game winning streak for the Magic. He led that 21-point win against the Sacramento Kings. After that, Orlando beat the Atlanta Hawks by 41 massive points. Then, in what was the final game of an eventful 1992 for O'Neal, he had his second 20-20 game in a loss to the LA Lakers. He finished that game with 23 points and 23 rebounds.

In his first game in the New Year of 1993, Shaquille O'Neal would feel the physicality of the Bad Boys Detroit Pistons team that, despite being in the twilight of its time as a powerhouse squad, was still very much playing the same brutal defense. The Magic would lose that game while Shaq finished with 29 points and 15 rebounds.

O'Neal would see Michael Jordan on the other end of the court for the first time in his professional career. He was an intimidating force on the defensive end but would fail to secure a win for the Magic. Four days later on January 16, they saw the Chicago Bulls again. This time, O'Neal came out with the win after registering 29 points, 24 rebounds, and five blocks against the defending champions. But he was merely a witness to Michael Jordan going for a ridiculous 64-point performance to steal the attention that night.

Two days later, Shaq would post a new career high in points against the Philadelphia 76ers. Versus no less than the 7'7" center Manute Bol,

Superman used his power against the lanky skyscraper to register 38 points, 16 rebounds, and eight blocks in a loss. Five days later, he tied that performance when he had 38 points, 13 rebounds, and seven blocks against the Dallas Mavericks. He would miss only two of his 16 shots that night.

It would take nearly a month for Shaquille O'Neal to eclipse his career high in points. In a loss to the Detroit Pistons on February 16, he had 46 points, 21 rebounds, and five blocks in overtime. At that time, Shaq already knew he was voted into the All-Star Game as a starter. He even topped the Eastern Conference in votes, eclipsing a favorite superstar, Michael Jordan.

Shaq's All-Star start did not sit well with the New York Knicks' Pat Riley, who was going to coach the Eastern Conference All-Stars that year. He thought that no rookie should be able to start in the midseason classic and that his player, Patrick Ewing, should have gotten the nod over O'Neal. He ended up playing Shaq and Ewing the same amount of minutes to the dismay of the rookie All-Star.[iii]

A few games after the midseason classic, Shaq would face David Robinson for the first time in his career as the Magic welcomed the San Antonio Spurs. Robinson not only came out with the win but would beat O'Neal concerning performance. He had 23 points, 16 rebounds, seven assists, four steals, and three blocks. Meanwhile, O'Neal a tough 19-point and 13-rebound outing against a man he grew up watching.

46

The next time Shaq would face The Admiral, he would again get outplayed in another Orlando Magic loss on March 19. He would finish with only 15 points and 13 rebounds while Robinson had 30 points on him. Just two games before that, he had another tough night against Hakeem Olajuwon, who he was still unable to stop on the defensive end because of his inexperience defending elite centers.

As the season was nearing its end, O'Neal would have back-to-back 20-20 outings for a Magic team that was trying to get a playoff spot. Shaq first registered 20 points and 21 rebounds in a win over the Boston Celtics on April 18. Two days later, he had 20 points and a new career high 25 rebounds against a Washington Bullets team that he was bullying all season long.

The highlight of the season for O'Neal was on April 23 in a win against the New Jersey Nets. Opposing big man Derrick Coleman was talking trash to Shaq all night long and even threatened to dunk on the rookie. That was the biggest mistake he would ever make in his life because Shaq had his eyes on him the entire night. In one play, when Shaq was struggling all game long, the large rookie received a pass near the basket on the weak side to get open for a dunk. O'Neal dunked the ball so hard while dragging Coleman with him that the entire backboard was collapsing before his very eyes. The shot clock nearly even hit him on the head if it were not for his reflexes.[iii]

As the backboard and rim were crashing down, the New Jersey crowd cheered for something they have probably never seen before.

Shaquille O'Neal, with all his strength and weight, pulled the entire basket down. It was a show of power and dominance for O'Neal as if he was telling the whole league that no other player in the history of the NBA could do what he does. After that season, the NBA began reinforcing the baskets to prevent similar incidents from happening again. That was one of the ways Shaquille O'Neal changed the game. You know a player is dominant when the league adjusts for him.

After his rookie season, Shaquille O'Neal had already established himself as a legitimate beast of an NBA center. He averaged 23.4 points, 13.9 rebounds, and 3.5 blocks. He also shot 56.2% from the floor and was proving to be an unstoppable scoring machine inside the paint. Shaq would win the Rookie of the Year award and became the first rookie in 11 years to have 1,000 points and 1,000 rebounds.[iii] But Shaq would not win Rookie of the Year unanimously because the likes of Alonzo Mourning and Christian Laettner would also have good rookie seasons. He would then lead the Orlando Magic to a 41-41 season. That was a 21-game improvement from the previous year, though they would miss the postseason.

While Shaquille O'Neal had a dominant rookie season that would even surpass what veteran centers could do at their best state, the young Superman was still far from his dominant self. Shaq would find out the hard way that he had trouble defending and going up against elite centers. Whenever he faced the likes of Olajuwon, Ewing, or Robinson, his numbers would drop.

It was not because Shaq was not bigger or stronger than other elite centers. He rarely faced players that could match his size and strength. It was a matter of experience. O'Neal had met centers that were probably bigger and stronger than the elite ones in the NBA. But none of them were even close to the skill and experience that the likes of Olajuwon and Robinson had. O'Neal found out that experience was his best teacher as he was going to gear up for more seasons of banging against the NBA's best big men.

Teaming Up With Penny

During the offseason of 1993, the Orlando Magic had a nearly impossible chance of landing the number one pick in the upcoming NBA Draft. Despite a 1 out of 66 chance of getting the pick, they managed to win the pick to the delight of Shaquille O'Neal, who wanted the Orlando Magic to give him another star to team up with.[iii] The Magic could not do it with Shaq alone, but they were one star away from actually competing for a title.

Originally, the Orlando Magic front office wanted to draft Chris Webber to add another capable big man to their already dominant frontline. But Shaq had another idea. He wanted to team up with a star guard and told the team general manager to draft Anfernee "Penny" Hardaway, who he became close with while doing a movie together. He wanted Hardaway because of the guard's playmaking and scoring abilities.

The Magic would not heed O'Neal's demands of selecting Hardaway with the top pick and would instead strategically draft Chris Webber. Knowing that the Golden State Warriors wanted Webber and that they wanted to bring over the third pick Penny into Orlando, the Magic traded the top draft pick to acquire Hardaway and three future first round picks. This not only gave the Magic a chance to satisfy O'Neal, but it also allowed them to bring in younger players in the future because of the trade.

Shaq and Penny had a good relationship together and both competed well to make each other better. Penny would come in playing the shooting guard spot while Scott Skiles was there to mentor him and to cede the starting point guard spot to him later. With another terrific passer, a new coach, and an improved and more experienced Shaq, the Orlando Magic were rearing to become contenders in the East.

In only his first game of the season, Shaquille O'Neal immediately dominated. In only 31 minutes of play in a blowout win against the Miami Heat, Shaq made 17 of his 24 shots to end up with 42 points in addition to 12 rebounds. But he was not done. Shaq would lead the Magic to a 25-point win against the Philadelphia 76ers by posting 36 points and five blocks in another dominant effort. And then, on November 9, he would post 37 points in a win against the Indiana Pacers.

In just his first three games of the season, Shaquille O'Neal showed that he wanted to be the new dominant star in the NBA as the league was still finding the next face of basketball since Michael Jordan had just retired after winning three straight titles for the Bulls. Shaq averaged 38.3 points on a ridiculous 72% shooting clip from the floor. He did that all in only 33 minutes of play in those three wins for the Magic.

While O'Neal would slow down a little as the season progressed, he would score at least 40 points for the second time when Orlando lost to Boston on November 19. Shaq had 41 points in addition to 10 rebounds that night. But O'Neal was not done. A night later, he was an all-around defensive beast in a dominant effort against the New Jersey Nets. In only 36 minutes of play, Shaq protected the paint and intimidated all comers to register a new career and franchise high of 15 blocks. Shaq tied the record for second all-time in most blocks in a single game. Elmore Smith holds the record with 17 blocks. In addition to his 15 rejections, O'Neal also had 24 points and a new career high 28 rebounds for his first ever triple-double in the NBA.

On December 9, Shaquille O'Neal would have a new career high in points. In 45 minutes of play in a loss to the Indiana Pacers, Shaq finished with 49 points while impressively missing only three of his 18 free throw attempts that night. That game was in the middle of what was to become an 18-game stretch of consecutive double-doubles for Superman. O'Neal averaged 27.6 points and nearly 14 rebounds in those 18 games. And with the help of a passer like Hardaway, who could also attract the defense away from O'Neal,

Shaq was making 60% of his shots and had seven games of scoring at least 30 points during that run.

In the middle of January 1994, O'Neal would have one of the best five-game stretches of his early career. He would average about 35 points on 70.5% shooting while rebounding 13 misses a game in those five consecutive outings of scoring at least 30 points. He had another game of scoring at least 40 points in that stretch. Shaq finished with 40 points and 19 rebounds in a dominant effort against the Clippers on January 19.

In the middle of February, after he made another start for the East in the All-Star Game, Shaquille O'Neal had two consecutive 30-20 games. He first posted 36 points and 24 rebounds (14 offensive boards) against the Boston Celtics on February 15. Three days later, he would go for 38 points and 20 rebounds in a dominant win over the Seattle SuperSonics.

Shaq's fifth game of scoring at least 40 points came on March 3 in a win against the Dallas Mavericks. O'Neal finished that game with 43 points and 16 rebounds. He had a similar feat six days later after posting 40 points and 14 rebounds in a win against the Sixers. In his next game, which was against the same team, he dominated the Sixers again by posting 28 points and 21 rebounds.

Against the Mavericks in another monstrous effort against a weaker frontline on March 16, Shaquille O'Neal had another 30-20 game. He posted 34 points and 21 rebounds in addition to the five blocks he had in that match. Two days later, he dominated the Cleveland Cavaliers with 38 points and 15 rebounds. Performances like those made people believe that Shaq was indeed becoming the most unstoppable player in the entire NBA.

O'Neal saved his best performances in the month of April when the Orlando Magic were trying to vie for one of the top playoff spots in the Eastern Conference. In a game against the Pistons early in the month, Shaq had 40 points to mark the sixth time he had at least 40 markers. Then on April 15, he posted 42 points in a double-overtime loss to the Celtics. But just when the season was about to end, O'Neal demolished the Minnesota Timberwolves frontline (along with college rival Christian Laettner) for 53 points on 22 out of 31 shooting from the field. He did that in only 36 minutes of play in a win against Laettner, who only had 6 points. That was how far Shaq had already widened the gap between himself and the man who was considered the better player in college. Shaq would end the season with a 30-20 effort by going for 32 points and 22 rebounds against the Nets.

At the end of the season, Shaquille O'Neal improved by leaps and bounds thanks to how Hardaway was making it easier for him on the offensive end along with the additions he had in his own game. O'Neal averaged 29.3 points, 13.2 rebounds, and 2.9 blocks the entire season. He led the league in shooting percentage by making 60% of his shots. He was also the most efficient scorer in the league after leading the NBA in effective field goal percentage. Shaq was also the league's second leading scorer after David Robinson narrowly beat him for the award.

Despite enormous numbers posted by O'Neal, the abundance of centers during that era of the NBA would have Shaq finish the season as only the league's third best center after he was selected to the All-NBA Third Team. 1994 league MVP Hakeem Olajuwon was selected First Team. Meanwhile, league-leading scorer David Robinson was Second Team. O'Neal would, however, lead the Magic to the fourth seed in the East with a 50-32 record.

Shaquille O'Neal would make his playoff debut on April 28, 1994, against the Indiana Pacers in the first round of the postseason. However, playing against a team that had a bevy of big men to throw at him in the likes of towering Dutchman Rik Smits and young big men Dale Davis and Antonio Davis, Shaq struggled all game long for his 24 points and 19 rebounds. The Magic would drop that first home game.

It was even harder for O'Neal in Game 2. He struggled to go 3 out of 8 from the field while opposing big men denied him possessions and position. He finished with only 15 points in another loss for Orlando. The Indiana Pacers would complete the sweep in Game 3, where Shaq had 23 points and 14 rebounds. O'Neal's first three playoff games were far from how he dominated the regular season. He merely averaged 20.7 points and 13.3 rebounds during the postseason. Despite the struggles in the playoffs, the future was bright for Orlando considering that Shaq was still improving and that Penny Hardaway proved to be a stellar secondary choice for the Magic.

First Finals Appearance

The Orlando Magic would add key pieces to their lineup to help what was becoming the next great NBA duo in Shaquille O'Neal and Penny Hardaway. They would sign point guard Brian Shaw after Scott Skiles left the team primarily because of an altercation with Shaq. The next key addition was Horace Grant, who was the third head behind Jordan and Pippen when the Bulls won three straight championships from 1991 to 1993. With the added experience and firepower on the roster, the Magic were becoming favorites to win it all in the East.

Early in the season, it became clear that Shaq was out there on the floor looking for blood and wanting to become the most dominant force in the NBA. One of his best games at that juncture was his first ever 40-20 game. In just his third game of the season and against the Charlotte Hornets, O'Neal dominated Alonzo Mourning under the basket and on the boards. He went for 46 points, which he scored mostly on putbacks thanks to the 14 offensive rebounds he collected in the game. In addition to the win, he also had 20 total rebounds in that match. And while the Magic would lose their next game a night later on November 10, O'Neal finished with a consecutive dominant 40-point performance when he finished with 41 markers against Ewing and the Knicks.

Shaquille O'Neal's third 40-point game came against the Sacramento Kings on November 30. He finished that night with 41 points and nine rebounds in another win for the Magic. The Orlando Magic could not stop winning early on in the season thanks to O'Neal and Hardaway, who was quickly becoming a star. In the first 20 games that Shaq played, Orlando would lose only four times. In those 20 games, O'Neal averaged 29.9 points on 60% shooting in addition to the 10.6 rebounds he was collecting.

In game number 21 for O'Neal for the season, he would go for his fourth 40-point outing by making 15 of his 20 shots in a win against the Golden State Warriors on December 16. He finished that night with 40 points and 18 rebounds. Performances like those in December made O'Neal one of the top performing players in that month. In 17 games in December, he averaged 29.2 points and 10.4 rebounds. He scored over 30 points nine times during that stretch. The Magic were 13-4 during that month.

In what was considered one of his most dominant stretch of games in just his third season in the NBA, Shaquille O'Neal would average 31.5 points and 12 rebounds in 12 games of pure monstrosity for the unstoppable force. He had eight games of scoring over 30 points in that stretch. Those included two games wherein he scored over 40 markers.

Shortly after leading the Eastern Conference All-Stars in scoring in the midseason classic wherein he was paired alongside first time All-

Star Penny Hardaway in the starting lineup, Shaq went for three straight games of scoring at least 30 points. He averaged nearly 35 points and nearly 11 rebounds in that stretch but would sustain a minor injury on February 24 against Boston.

Showing no signs of rust upon returning from injury on February 28, Shaquille O'Neal went for 41 points and ten rebounds against no less than Patrick Ewing and the New York Knicks in a battle of two of the best centers in the league. A game later, Shaq helped defeat the Houston Rockets when he collected 20 rebounds against reigning league MVP, Hakeem Olajuwon.

On March 8 against a helpless Laker frontline, Shaquille O'Neal owned the paint and posted 46 points and 11 rebounds. That performance came after he posted two consecutive games of scoring at least 30 points. At that point of the season, the Orlando Magic were becoming favorites to lock in the top seed in the Eastern Conference while O'Neal was also becoming one of the top MVP candidates.

Late in the season when the Magic were trying to finish strong to secure the top seed in the East, O'Neal had 14 consecutive double-double performances while averaging 29.4 points and 14.1 rebounds in the process. He had seven games of scoring at least 30 points in that stretch. In one of those outings, he had 40 points and 19 rebounds when the Magic defeated the Pistons on April 5.

In his third season in the NBA, Shaquille O'Neal averaged a league-leading 29.3 points to go along with 11.4 rebounds and 2.4 blocks.

That was the first of two scoring titles for the dominant big man. Shaq would then lead the Magic to a franchise best 57-win season to lock in the Eastern Conference's top seed heading into the postseason.

While Shaq and Hardaway were the main reasons as to why the Magic led the Eastern Conference, it was the team's overall effort that made them a top team in the league. The new additions added firepower to a team that ran the floor hard every possession. Everybody on the team ran. That included Shaq himself, who was like a gazelle on steroids at that early part of his career when he was a leaner and more athletic version of himself. The Magic led the league in offensive rating, was one of the top three-point shooting squads, and was the league's highest scoring team thanks to a bevy of shooters that surrounded Shaq all over the perimeter.

Unfortunately for Shaq, one other center in the league was performing better than he was. David Robinson of the San Antonio Spurs led his team to the league's best record that season. Robinson, with 73 first place votes and a total of 901 points, would win the MVP award over Shaquille O'Neal. Shaq finished with 12 first place votes and a total of 605 points as the runner-up to Robinson in the award voting. Shaq would also finish behind Robinson as the second best center in the NBA after having been selected to the All-NBA Second Team. Nevertheless, what was more important for O'Neal was that he and the Orlando Magic were in the best shape to compete for the NBA championship that year.

Shaq's road towards his first Finals appearance would start against the Boston Celtics in the opening round of the 1995 NBA playoffs. Despite a valiant effort from the Celtics' big man in limiting O'Neal's efficiency, the self-proclaimed Superman of the NBA still finished with 23 points and 11 rebounds in what became a brutal 47-point rout for the Orlando Magic. However, they would fail to replicate the same performance when they would lose Game 2. Shaq had 22 points and nine rebounds that night.

In Game 3 in Boston, Shaquille O'Neal would have his first playoff 20-20 game after finishing the win with 20 points and 21 rebounds. Two days later, he would help the Magic finish the Celtics up by hitting 60% of his shots from the floor. O'Neal had 25 points and 13 rebounds in Game 4. He averaged 22.5 points and 13.5 rebounds in his and the Orlando Magic's first playoff series win.

The second round would not be easy for him and teammate Horace Grant, who played for the Bulls just a season back. The Orlando Magic would face the Chicago Bulls, who had just gotten Michael Jordan back from retirement a few months ago. Though the 1994-95 Chicago Bulls team was still trying to figure things out with Jordan back, they were still the overall best team during the 90's era and were still three-time champions at that time.

Game 1 would start in Orlando, where O'Neal dominated the weaker Chicago frontline. Shaq made 7 of his 11 shots from the floor and 12 of his 16 free throws to finish the game with 26 points to go along with the 12 boards he collected. The Bulls, however, would steal Game 2 away from the Magic much like how the Celtics did in the previous round. Saddled with foul trouble, Shaq played only 33 minutes that night but still had 25 points and 12 rebounds.

In Game 3, the Orlando Magic would regain homecourt advantage, and the series lead when they beat the Bulls in Chicago. Shaq finished that night with 28 points and ten rebounds. But despite what could have been his first playoff triple-double, O'Neal would fail to take a 3-1 lead when they lost in Game 4. He finished that game with 17 points, ten rebounds, and nine assists.

Shaquille O'Neal came back strong in Game 5. He was relentless on the offensive boards despite struggling from the field. Though O'Neal shot only 35%, he collected 14 big rebounds on the offensive end to finish with a rebound total of 22. He then had five blocks in addition to 23 points to lead the Magic to within one win away from the Eastern Conference Finals. O'Neal and the Magic would then have the honor of being the only team to beat the Jordan-led Bulls in a playoff series from 1991 until 1998 when he finished with 27 points and 13 rebounds in Game 6.

Coming into the East Finals full of confidence after beating Michael Jordan and his Bulls, Shaq would have his first 30-point playoff performance against the much taller Rik Smits of the Indiana Pacers. He paced the win over Indiana with 32 big points and 11 rebounds. In

Game 2, he had an even better night by going for 39 points and ten rebounds to take a 2-0 series lead.

Somehow, the Indiana Pacers fought back at home and hounded O'Neal down in the paint to limit his offensive performance as well as his minutes on the floor. Shaq combined for only 34 points and 16 rebounds in both Games 3 and 4 as the Magic were heading back to Orlando tied with the Pacers 2-2 in the series.

Shaq went back to work in Game 5. He posted 35 big points to go along with ten rebounds to give the series lead back to the Orlando Magic. But the Pacers protected home court yet again when they won in Game 6. But homecourt advantage proved too critical for the Magic in Game 7 when the entire team rode a frenzied crowd to rout the Pacers by 24 points. In an overall team effort, O'Neal had 25 points and 11 rebounds that evening on his way to his first ever NBA Finals appearance.

The NBA Finals would prove to be Shaquille O'Neal's toughest test at that point in his career. The sixth-seeded Houston Rockets had just beaten the San Antonio Spurs, who held the best record in the NBA, back in the Western Conference Finals. Posting 35 points and 12.3 rebounds the entire series against the Spurs, Hakeem Olajuwon proved that he was still the NBA's best center by demolishing the MVP David Robinson, who could not defend him nor even score against him. Coming into the 1995 NBA Finals, Olajuwon was out for blood and was at the best form of his entire career, and he was not willing to cede his throne as the best big man in the NBA to a young 23-year-old Shaquille O'Neal.

Shaquille O'Neal, ever the competitive man, was not intimidated by his more accomplished matchup. He would lead the Orlando Magic to a 20-point in the second quarter, and it seemed like his team was on its way to a dominant win. But Olajuwon and new Rocket member Clyde Drexler led a comeback that was punctuated when the Magic's Nick Anderson failed to make four free throws in the dying seconds of the game. Shaq had a near triple-double night of 26 points, 16 rebounds, and nine assists. However, Olajuwon outscored him with some of the most beautiful post moves in basketball history. He had 32 over O'Neal.

The Magic's fortunes did not change the entire series. Shaquille O'Neal looked like he could not defend Hakeem Olajuwon. To his defense, nobody in the entire league could have been able to guard Olajuwon at that point in his career. Hakeem abused Shaq and all other Magic defenders in the paint while holding his own against the much bigger and stronger center.

In the end, the Orlando Magic looked disheartened as it was only O'Neal that performed well. But not even he could outplay Hakeem Olajuwon, who led a Houston Rockets sweep over the Magic. Shaq had impressive numbers of 28 points, 12.5 rebounds, and 6.3 assists during the four-game series. He even shot nearly 60% from the floor. But Olajuwon outscored him in every game of the series and did not have a single game where he was held under 30 points. Hakeem had 32.8 points, 11.5 rebounds, and 5.5 assists against Shaq the entire series to win the Finals MVP.

In retrospect, Shaquille O'Neal said that he had so much respect of Hakeem Olajuwon that he was not as aggressive as he would have wanted to be during that series.[iii] But he would also admit that Olajuwon was the only player that time he could not intimidate.[vi] Shaq could trash talk and intimidate the likes of Ewing, Malone, Robinson, and every other big man in the league. But Hakeem was so laser focused that not even O'Neal's sheer size, strength, and trash talking could break him. But despite the loss, Shaq was still only 23 years old and had just learned valuable lessons and experiences during that run to the 1995 NBA Finals.

Feud With Penny, Final Season in Orlando

In just three seasons removed from college, Shaquille O'Neal had already established himself as the franchise's single best player in its history. But Shaq's status as a star transcended Orlando. He was one of the league's brightest premier players. At the tender age of 23 years old, the league had seen its next megastar when players like Jordan, Malone, Barkley, and Olajuwon would finally decide to hang their sneakers up. His dominance on the floor and ability to lead a team to victories were what made Shaq arguably the biggest asset in the NBA considering his youth, size, and marketability.

But within the Orlando Magic organization, one other player was quickly becoming a star in his right. That was Penny Hardaway, who was just as young as Shaq was and had just become an All-Star in only his second season in the NBA. At that point, people were calling Penny the next Magic. At 6'7", he had size at the point guard position. He ran the floor hard every play and could make passes that were reminiscent of Johnson. Hardaway was an up-and-coming star that was the right fit for a dominant big man like Shaquille O'Neal.

Initially, there were no problems with O'Neal and Hardaway's partnership. Shaq was the first option on offense, like he would have been on any other team. Meanwhile, Penny's purpose was to be a secondary scorer and the team's primary facilitator to help get his teammates open looks. In essence, both players were nearly equally invaluable to the Orlando Magic.

The problem came when Penny Hardaway wanted his contract renewed. He wanted to get paid big. There were no problems regarding that. He was a terrific player that needed to get paid with an amount similar to what the league's biggest stars were getting. But he wanted more. He believed he should be getting more than what the Orlando Magic were offering O'Neal for his contract extension. For Hardaway, he was the more valuable player in Orlando.[iii]

While Shaquille O'Neal agreed that Penny Hardaway deserved a big contract, he had problems with his point guard believing that he was the alpha male in Orlando. Shaq had the numbers, awards, and accomplishments to prove that he was the main man on the roster. But for Penny, the Magic was "his" team and that he thought that O'Neal was the Robin to his Batman.

With egos clashing and with both players believing they were the top man on the Orlando Magic roster, the chemistry between Shaq and Penny was never the same after that. But with the way the Magic were playing that season, it was not even apparent to the naked eye that there was a tarnished relationship between O'Neal and Hardaway. But Penny had a case for himself because he would keep the Magic afloat in the first two months of the 1995-96 season when Shaq was out with a thumb injury. Orlando would merely lose five of their first 23 games without O'Neal.

Shaq would return to action on December 15 and dominated like he did not miss a beat. He posted 26 points and 11 rebounds in only 24 minutes in that win over the Utah Jazz. Orlando would win eight of their first nine games with O'Neal back in the lineup. In those nine games, Shaq scored over 30 points thrice. His season high at that time was when he had 38 points in a blowout win against the Seattle SuperSonics. He played only 33 minutes in that dominant effort.

Injuries would nevertheless keep Shaquille O'Neal in and out of the lineup as the season progressed. But they never hindered him from posting huge numbers whenever he was on the floor playing. One of his best performances during those injury-laden stretches was when he had 30 points, 19 rebounds, seven assists, and five blocks in a win over the Boston Celtics on January 30.

Missing games and playing at less than a hundred percent the entire season did not hinder Shaquille O'Neal from making his fourth consecutive All-Star appearance. With 25 points and ten rebounds that night, Shaq was the Eastern Conference All-Stars' leading scorer and leading rebounder in that win over the West. But somehow, Michael Jordan still came out of the event as the All-Star MVP.

The middle of the season seemed like enough for Shaq to return to his unstoppable self. Right after the All-Star Game, he posted three straight games of scoring at least 30 points while collecting double-digit rebounds. All three of those games were wins for the Magic.

Early on March 2, 1996, O'Neal would have his season high of 41 points in addition to the 17 rebounds he collected in a blowout win against the Portland Trailblazers. But that was not his best performance for the season because, 20 days later, he topped it off by going for 49 points and 17 rebounds in a win over the Washington Bullets. Shaq would then end his final ten games of the regular season scoring at least 30 points in four outings.

At the end of his fourth NBA season, Shaquille O'Neal averaged 26.6 points and 11 rebounds while playing only 54 games the entire season. The Orlando Magic would win a franchise record 60 games and held their own even when O'Neal was injured. This only bolstered Penny's case as the Magic's alpha player after he led Orlando to a 20-8 record in the 28 games that O'Neal missed. He even finished third in the MVP voting behind Michael Jordan and David Robinson.

Though the Orlando Magic had a dominant season and would have turned heads their way, most of the attention went to the Chicago Bulls after they won a then-record 72 games. Because of that, the Magic failed to replicate their previous season when they were the top seed in the Eastern Conference heading into the playoffs.

Being second seed did not stop the Magic from dominating the early rounds of the playoffs, especially when Shaquille O'Neal was already back in top shape. Orlando quickly swept the Detroit Pistons in the opening round even when O'Neal was not putting up dominant numbers. He only had 13 points in the series-clinching win and did not have a double-double the entire series.

The Orlando Magic stayed the course even in the second round when they had an easy series against the Atlanta Hawks. O'Neal opened things up by going for 41 points and 13 rebounds in a Game 1 blowout win. He then contributed 28 points on 11 out of 15 shooting in what was a 26-point blowout in Game 2. The Magic then went up to an insurmountable 3-0 lead after winning Game 2. Shaq had 24 points and 12 rebounds in that game. Atlanta managed to get a win in Game 4, but Shaq's 27 points and 15 rebounds in Game 5 did them in.

As smooth as the first two rounds for Shaq and the Magic were, the Eastern Conference Finals were the end of the joyride for them. The Chicago Bulls would end up sweeping them that series by playing their brand of tough, hard-nosed defense on all of the Orlando Magic's players. This included Shaq, who had abused the Bulls' inside defense a year ago.

The difference between the previous season and that year versus the Bulls was that Chicago had Dennis Rodman. Shaq was abusing the Bulls' seven footers in the lane. With no one else to stop Superman, Chicago went to the 6'8" lean defensive and rebound specialist Dennis Rodman. Rodman would use all of the strength he had in his body to try to push O'Neal out of the paint even before the big man could get the ball in a good position. Though Shaq still had an excellent series on the offensive end, Rodman made him work for it. O'Neal was even outrebounded by the smaller Dennis Rodman the entire series and was getting pushed out of the paint and kept off the boards. And unfortunately for Shaq, he would never get the chance to take his vengeance as a Magic player. He had played his final series for Orlando in that loss to the Bulls.

The Move to LA

Shaquille O'Neal held out extending his contract with the Orlando Magic the entire 1995-96 season until he became a free agent in the offseason of 1996 after the Bulls won the NBA title. At that time, free agents could sign with any team they wanted. Rules were different. Rookie contracts could not restrict the player after their deal was over with their original team. Shaq was ripe for the open market and was literally and figuratively the biggest free agent that offseason.

O'Neal intended to stay with the Orlando Magic. He loved the organization. However, the front office low-balled him with a contract too cheap for a player of his caliber. They initially offered him a seven-year $69 million contract. But O'Neal knew he was worth more. Other players during that offseason were getting deals north of $100 million. Shaq was a lot better and more accomplished than those guys. He was worth more than $69 million.

Orlando's final offer to Shaquille O'Neal was $80 million. Meanwhile, players like Juwan Howard and Alonzo Mourning were getting more than him from other teams. While money was not the real issue for Shaq, what convinced him to leave Orlando was that the Magic front office did not want to give him what he was worth because they did not want to hurt Penny Hardaway's feelings if they gave O'Neal more money.[iii]

Everything went back to the alpha male feud between O'Neal and Hardaway. It was never about the money, as former teammate Horace Grant would say. It was all about the ego between the two players.[vii] Shaq was the established franchise player, whose alpha male and leadership status was unquestioned. Meanwhile, Penny was an up-and-coming star that showed his ability to lead the team with an injured O'Neal the last season.

Here comes Jerry West of the Los Angeles Lakers offering Shaquille O'Neal $98 million for seven years. After all the negative publicity that Shaq was getting with his negotiations with the Orlando Magic, he was ready to take the offer that West gave him. But West called again and said that they had just freed up cap space and were willing to give O'Neal $121 million, which was a league record at that time.

When the contract was signed, Shaq and Penny were in Atlanta for the 1996 Olympics. O'Neal never told Hardaway that he had just signed with the Lakers as West himself told the big guy they were going to win a lot of titles together with his 18-year-old teenager, who he thought would become the best player in the world someday. News broke out, and Penny felt blindsided and betrayed. The entire city of Orlando felt betrayed as well. But O'Neal kept insisting it was never about money.[iii] It was about his ego and how he and Penny did not see eye-to-eye on who should have been the alpha male on the team.

Penny Hardaway would end up staying with the Magic. He would lead the team to two more playoff appearances, but injuries would eventually take their toll on him and would make him a shell of his former self. In hindsight when the two players were in an interview several years later, Hardaway admitted he could have avoided the injuries if he did not have to shoulder the entire load himself. Meanwhile, O'Neal said he could have handled things differently with Penny and Orlando if he had been given a second chance.[viii] But at that moment in time back in 1996, O'Neal had just become a Laker and was on his way to Los Angeles to live the Hollywood life.

First Season as a Laker, Meeting Kobe Bryant

When O'Neal became a Laker, his primary focus back then was to bring the title back to Los Angeles. But the process was long, especially when the West was always the more competitive conference. In fact, it took longer for him to get to the Finals as a Laker than when he was with the Orlando Magic. But O'Neal was patient. He wanted to win, but his love for the big city life in LA helped him become more patient.

That time, the Lakers had young talent mixed with some veteran leadership. Their talent level was even probably better than what O'Neal had in Orlando. The veterans that helped the team mature were Byron Scott, who was a member of the Showtime Lakers back in the 80's, and Jerome Kersey. Shaq also shared the paint with veteran big man Elden Campbell. The two guard spots were occupied by talented passer Nick Van Exel and two-way wingman Eddie Jones. But arguably their best young assets were two rookies that would soon bring in five titles to Los Angeles. The first one was Derek Fisher. The other one was the 18-year-old kid that Jerry West was raving about. Nevertheless, Shaq was the leader and the best player at that point in the Lakers' history. He immediately became The Man in LA.

In O'Neal's debut game with the Lakers, he made 8 of his ten shots to score 23 points in addition to the 14 boards he collected in that win against the Phoenix Suns. Then, in his second game, O'Neal showed that he was dominant in any uniform he would wear after going for his then-Laker highs of 35 points and 19 rebounds in a win against the Minnesota Timberwolves. Shaq would start his LA career with eight consecutive double-doubles.

To O'Neal's surprise, he was selected as one of the 50 Greatest Players of All Time even though he was still in his fifth season in the NBA. That showed how much the entire league valued what Shaq has done in just the early part of his life in the NBA. They also knew right then and there that Shaquille O'Neal would probably go down as one of the best to ever play once it was all said and done.

Shaq's first 20-20 outing in LA would come on November 22 when he had 29 points and 21 rebounds in a win against the Spurs. Four days later, he had another one after he posted 23 points and 20 rebounds in a dominant win against the Philadelphia 76ers. And barely a month later, Shaquille O'Neal would post a new season high when he went for 41 points in addition to the 13 rebounds he collected in a win against the Milwaukee Bucks.

Because of the public backlash of his decision to go to Los Angeles the past offseason, O'Neal would not be voted as an All-Star starter for the first time in his entire career. He would finish second behind Hakeem Olajuwon, who was already slowing down, in the voting for centers. Nevertheless, Shaq was still selected as an All-Star, but would have to miss the midseason classic for the first time in his career because of a knee injury that sidelined him for 28 consecutive games. He would also miss the ceremony for the 50 Greatest Players of All Time.

Shaq would return to action when the regular season was nearing its end. He had 24 points and 11 boards on April 11 in his return game against the Suns in a win. Two days later, he showed flashes of his peak form when he had 39 points and 13 rebounds in a win against the Utah Jazz before going for 42 big points and 12 rebounds on April 17 in a win against the Sacramento Kings.

At the end of his first season as a Laker, Shaquille O'Neal averaged 26.2 points, 12.5 rebounds, 3.1 assists, and 2.9 blocks while playing in pain from the injury he had. The Lakers won 56 games that year, but would have won more had O'Neal been healthy. Los Angeles lost 13 games in the 31 outings that O'Neal missed.

In the first game of the postseason when the Lakers met the Blazers, O'Neal opened up with 46 points and 11 rebounds. His 46 points were the most that any Laker had put up in nearly three decades. He followed up that Game 1 win with 30 points in Game 2 to give LA a 2-0 lead. Shaq would help dispatch the Trailblazers in Game 4 by going for 27 points.

In the second round, the Los Angeles Lakers met a Utah Jazz team aching to make the NBA Finals in what was one of the franchise's best seasons ever. But even then and there, O'Neal recognized that they were not ready to beat one of the all-time best teams ever assembled during the 90's era. They would fall in five games. But one of the highlights of that series for the Lakers was when, in a Game 5 that went into overtime, their 18-year-old rookie air-balled four shots but never lost confidence in himself.

Despite the loss in the playoffs, O'Neal was not surprised that his first season in LA did not translate to a title. After all, he was still favoring his knee and had lost confidence in it for a while that season. But there were also several other factors that made him feel like the Lakers were not yet ready to make a title run back then. It all boiled down to the coach and the personnel.

O'Neal loved then head coach Del Harris. Harris treated everyone on the team equally. However, Shaq thought that he was getting himself pushed over by front office and fans a lot. On top of that, Harris was also always butting heads with point guard Nick Van Exel.[iii]

Speaking of Van Exel, Shaq always felt like he was not the right fit. Van Exel was a good passer, but he was too busy trying to be a star instead of playing within the flow of the game. O'Neal knew that it was only a matter of time until Derek Fisher or some other future veteran point guard would take his place. Shaq also felt the same way with Eddie Jones, who he thought was not playing to his full potential because he knew that a younger and better player would soon take his place.[iii] That player was the 18-year-old teenager that everyone in the Laker front office was raving about.

At 18 years old, Kobe Bryant was the first guard taken straight out of high school for a long while. He was a steal in the 1996 NBA Draft after several teams slept on him because they were unsure of what he would bring at his age. But West knew how talented the kid was when he worked out for the Lakers before the draft. He even claimed that Bryant was better than everyone they had in the locker room. Of course, they have not yet signed O'Neal back then. The Lakers had so much trust in Bryant that they traded a proven center Vlade Divac on draft night for Kobe.

Shaq remembered how skinny Kobe was when he first got to LA. Back then, there was no Shaq-Kobe combo. Bryant was a kid fresh out of high school and had little life experience. But what he lacked back then in heft and experience, he more than made up for in confidence and work ethic. The trust in Bryant and the work ethic he had were too palpable not to be noticed.

Shaquille O'Neal already noticed how confident and hard-working Bryant was early in his rookie year. Kobe often told Shaq that he would someday become one of the best scorers in the league and would have multiple championships to boot. History would tell us how that turned out. O'Neal also saw that Kobe Bryant outworked everyone else on the roster. He would be at the facility three hours before the scheduled practice. He was practicing shots on his own and was even doing moves pretending he had a ball in his hands. It was back then and there when O'Neal knew that this 18-year-old teenage kid was going to be something else in the NBA.[iii]

But Bryant, as well as Shaq, struggled in their first season in Los Angeles. Shaq had to deal with injuries and the backlash of his decision to sign with LA. Meanwhile, Kobe Bryant was still not yet ready to take the league by storm. He was the one that air balled all those shots in that Game 5 overtime loss to the Jazz in the playoffs. When people jeered on Kobe for missing all those shots, it was O'Neal who gave the kid back his confidence by telling him that he would soon be the last person to laugh at all those who used to doubt him.[iii] Pretty soon, all of those jeers would turn into jeers for the young man people often called Shaq's "sidekick" in that Los Angeles Lakers era.

The Rise of Kobe Bryant, Shaq's Frustrations

Shaquille O'Neal continued to be his unstoppable self during the 1997-98 season. The Lakers also made a few adjustments to suit the demands of their franchise player. Instead of pairing Shaq with fellow center Campbell in the paint, Harris opted to start stretch forward Robert Horry instead. They also added Rick Fox, a key veteran defensive asset out on the perimeter. The 19-year-old Kobe Bryant also began seeing more minutes and getting more touches.

Shaq would once again start the season strong but would end up getting injured in the middle of November. He would miss the rest of the month as well as all of December because of the injury. And as always, he seemed as if he never lost a beat when he came back at the start of January 1998. O'Neal immediately returned to his superstar self and saw a return to the All-Star Game's starting lineup.

But Shaq was not the only Laker that was featured in that year's All-Star Game. Both Eddie Jones and Nick Van Exel were selected by coaches to participate in the midseason classic. And at the age of 19, Kobe Bryant became the youngest All-Star starter in the history of the league after his adoring fans voted him though. But he was still a thousand miles away from his superstar peak form. Surprisingly, Bryant edged out more established stars such as John Stockton, Jason Kidd, and Clyde Drexler for that starting spot. That was how fast the kid was becoming popular, probably because people already saw flashes of the great MJ in him. Kobe would have tons of duels with Michael Jordan in that All-Star Game.

Shaquille O'Neal was in MVP form after the All-Star Weekend. He would average 29 points and 11 rebounds in those 37 games. There were also three instances when he scored over 40 points in that run. He had 44 in a loss to Seattle on February 13. Then, on April 2, he dominated with 50 points against the New Jersey Nets. In the second to final game of the regular season, O'Neal dropped 43 points in only 33 minutes of play in a blowout win against the Dallas Mavericks.

At the end of the season, Shaq averaged 28.3 points, 11.4 rebounds, and 2.4 blocks. He also led the league in field goal shooting by going for 58.4% from the floor. O'Neal, having no other competition at the center position as Olajuwon, Ewing, and Robinson were beginning to slow down, was First Team All-NBA for the first time in his career. Shaq would also finish fourth in the MVP voting. Meanwhile, the rising Kobe Bryant averaged more than 15 points per game as a sixth man but would fail to win the Sixth Man of the Year award. And though the Lakers won 61 games, which was the most that O'Neal had won at that point in his career, they were only the third seed in the West behind the Jazz and the Sonics.

As expected of them, the Los Angeles Lakers steamrolled through the first two rounds of the playoffs. They defeated the Trailblazers in four games. After that, they dispatched the Sonics in only five outings. They had only lost twice in the playoffs on their way to the Western Conference Finals. However, in the West Finals, they were swept out of the title contention in only four games.

Shaquille O'Neal was so frustrated after that loss that he began to trash everything in the Lakers' bathroom. The man was a rampaging giant, and nobody wanted to go near him to try to calm him down. The only man brave enough was Jerry West, who told O'Neal he was acting like a child. West told Shaq the story of how he went to the Finals eight times but would only win the title in his ninth appearance. He said it always frustrated him, but he never acted the way O'Neal did in that bathroom.

Shaq got the picture. Jerry West was telling him to become a better leader and a role model to the younger guys amidst all of the frustration he was getting when he kept on losing year after year.

Nobody wanted to lose. But in Shaq's case, his competitiveness and desire to become the best made losing tougher to bear than the ordinary player. O'Neal would eventually calm down after realizing that acting like a child would not help him win a title.

The Chicago Bulls would eventually beat the Utah Jazz in the 1998 NBA Finals. Michael Jordan would call it a career for the second time in his life and would leave the throne of the NBA wide open for any superstar and team to take by force. But no player or team could do it until February of 1999 because of the NBA lockout, which was induced by certain labor disputes. The season started too late. There were no All-Star Weekend festivities while the regular season was cut short to 50 games.

Because of the long offseason, Shaquille O'Neal thought that everyone was out of shape. Apart from Kobe Bryant, players were lethargic and were getting fat. Shaq himself was not spared. It was around that time when O'Neal began growing larger than the 300-pound athletic freak that he was when he first got to the league. O'Neal started packing on serious mass and weight to the point that everyone that stood beside him looked like mere children to the hulking giant with a body so wide it could engulf the entire paint. But in Shaq's defense, his conditioning was the same. He may have slowed down and stopped running the floor as a guard would, but he also became more unstoppable inside the paint because of the added weight and mass that defenders had to deal with.

The Lakers needed a fresh start by firing Del Harris after 12 games. They would elevate assistant Kurt Rambis to the Head coaching spot. The problem that Shaq saw with Rambis was that he thought the new coach favored Kobe Bryant more than any other player. He made Kobe the golden boy of the team and would often forgive the youngster's childish and selfish plays out on the court.

While Shaq initially did not have personal problems with Kobe that time, the media blew the story up and reported that the two stars were not seeing eye-to-eye. But for O'Neal's part, it was all about basketball. The problems he and several other players had with Bryant was that he was not passing the ball enough and would instead settle for superstar highlight plays. But it was all about basketball. There was nothing personal. But if there was a cause to what would eventually become a feud between the two great players, one might trace it back to this point in time.

Shaq averaged 26.3 points and 10.7 rebounds that season. He still led the league in field goal percentage as well as effective field goal percentage that season, proving to the world that he was still the most efficient scorer in the entire league. However, he fell short to Allen Iverson for what would have been his second scoring title. That was also the season when Bryant fully blossomed into the Lakers' legitimate second option behind Shaq. Together, the two stars had 31 wins out of their 50 games that season.

In the first round of the playoffs, the Lakers steamrolled against a Houston Rockets team led by Scottie Pippen, Charles Barkley, and Hakeem Olajuwon who were all at the twilight years of their career. Using their superior youth and fresher legs, the Los Angeles Lakers defeated the team full of legends in only four games, proving that youth would sometimes beat out experience. That win was also retribution for Shaq, who lost to Hakeem's Rockets back in the 1995 NBA Finals.

But in the second round, the Lakers were swept out of the playoffs by the eventual champions, the San Antonio Spurs. Shaquille O'Neal gave all the credit to then-second year big man Tim Duncan for beating them. Like Olajuwon, Duncan was also one of the players that Shaq himself said he could never break. He could trash talk his way into mentally and emotionally beating other big men. But, to his account, Duncan would just play out there with a straight face while shooting bankers in his face. And on the defensive end, he would not also flinch against the much bigger man.[iii] That was the kind of focus and maturity that Shaq respected from his fellow big men.

After that embarrassing sweep at the hands of the Spurs, O'Neal's self-doubts began creeping into him again. He had already spent the same amount of seasons as he did with the Magic when he led Orlando to the NBA Finals in only his third season. But as a Laker, he was yet to step foot on the Promised Land. The media also began asking whether O'Neal could truly lead a team to a title.

Shaq thought to himself that it might not have been him or the personnel that kept the Lakers from winning a title. He was the most dominant player in the league that time and was arguably the best post-Jordan player of that era. He had a young and rising Kobe Bryant helping him out as the team's second option. They also brought in veteran help such as Glen Rice and Rick Fox with the heavy lifting. Instead, Shaq believed they needed a coach that could demand respect and reign in all of the roster's talent. The one man he had in mind was Phil Jackson. The Laker front office responded to the call by hiring the six-time NBA champion coach.

MVP Year, the Dawn of the Lakers Dynasty

Phil Jackson, the man that gave Michael Jordan six rings in Chicago, brought in the vaunted Triangle Offense the Bulls made so famous by dominating the 90's era. But the Chicago Bulls dynasty was over. Jackson was in LA to form a new dynasty there. He had a young kid that resembled Mike's game and maniacal passion for basketball. But what he did not have back in Chicago was a player that had the size and skill of Shaquille O'Neal.

Coming into the 1999-2000 season, one of the first things that Jackson asked Shaq to do was play at least 40 minutes a game because Wilt Chamberlain used to play nearly every single minute of a game back in the day. Before that season, O'Neal had never played 40 minutes a game the entire season. The most he played on average was 39.8 when he was a second-year player. But back then, he was young, full of energy, and lean. In his eighth season in the NBA, he was not getting any younger, had carried the load of two franchises already, and was a big pile of mass. There were also questions that arose about O'Neal's conditioning considering that he was already about 330 pounds at that time. But O'Neal would shatter that myth during the season.

Before the season started, the Lakers also added key pieces. Jones and Van Exel were already out of LA at that time. And instead of investing on multiple star-caliber players, the Lakers front office made sure that they filled the roster with guys that would fit the roster and would complement Shaq and Kobe. They added former champions John Salley and Ron Harper, who was an integral part of the Bulls dynasty. They also brought in Brian Shaw, one of Shaq's favorite teammates back in Orlando. And with big shot makers like Robert Horry, Rick Fox, and Glen Rice waiting outside for passes from O'Neal or Bryant, the Lakers were going to be title favorites that season.

Phil Jackson ran the triangle to perfection in LA. He made O'Neal the anchor of the system because of his post presence and his ability to make passes down low. The Triangle Offense stressed ball movement and cutting. Shaq was the perfect anchor because the amount of defense he attracted allowed players to cut or spot up for open shots. That was why most of the players surrounding Shaq and Kobe in LA that time were ones that could make open shots and were willing passers.

With the Lakers running the triangle under Phil and with Shaq in his prime while Kobe was at a young age with fresh legs, the Lakers were unstoppable. The Lakers would only lose four of their first 20 games that season. O'Neal was utterly dominant in most of those games. He posted 30 points and 20 rebounds in a win over Dallas on November 7. Then, against Phoenix eight days later, he had 34 points and 18 rebounds. He would then shoot 11 out of 13 from the field for 41 big points in addition to the 17 rebounds he collected and seven shots he blocked in a win against the Bulls on November 19. O'Neal would then score at least 30 points in the next three games after that performance.

Then, in the middle of December up to early January 2000, Shaq led the Lakers to a dominant 16-game winning streak. O'Neal had several impactful performances during that run. He had 38 points and 15 rebounds in a blowout win against the Clippers on January 4. The next night against the very same team, he posted 40 points and 19 rebounds. And in leading Los Angeles to their 16-game win streak, Shaq averaged 27.5 points and 15.4 rebounds. He scored at least 30 points seven times during that run and nearly had a triple-double of 31 points, 19 rebounds, and nine assists in a 35-point blowout against the Denver Nuggets in giving the Lakers win number 15.

After getting voted into the All-Star Game for the eighth time in his career, Shaq would win the All-Star MVP for the first time in his career after tallying 22 points and nine rebounds in a winning effort for the West. O'Neal would then lead the Lakers to a 19-game win streak after that All-Star break. During that run, Shaquille O'Neal averaged 30.3 points, 14.1 rebounds, 4.7 assists, and 2.7 blocks.

It was during that 19-game winning run when Shaquille O'Neal posted his best regular season game. In that dominant win over the Los Angeles Clippers, Shaq had 61 points and 23 rebounds. According to him, the reason as to why he was so inspired into demolishing the Clippers in that game was that he was denied complimentary tickets for his friends and family. The Clippers paid dearly for that.[iii]

After the 19-game win streak had ended, Shaq went on to average 34 points and 11 rebounds in his final 16 games of the regular season. The Lakers would only lose three times in those 16 games that Shaquille O'Neal played. Nobody could ever deny how great O'Neal was playing at that point of the season. He was not merely leading the Lakers in points and rebounds but also made sure that his team was on the top of the standings with the 67 wins he helped tally.

With a league-leading average of 29.7 points to go along with 13.6 rebounds, 3.8 assists, and three blocks, Shaquille O'Neal was named the NBA's Most Valuable Player after leading the Lakers to the league's best record. And proving that his added size and weight did not affect his conditioning, he logged in 40 minutes a game the entire season and did not seem like he was tired or gassed.

As O'Neal himself would recount, the first person he called upon receiving the award was his father, Sgt. Harrison, who he claimed could not contain his tears upon knowing that his son was named the league's top performing player that season. But Sarge would, later on, tell the big man that the MVP would be useless if there were no championship trophy at the end of the rainbow. He was right. For Shaq, it was championship or bust that season.[iii]

The Los Angeles Lakers opened the playoffs with a growing rival in the Sacramento Kings. At that point, it seemed as if the Lakers would quickly dispatch the Kings. After all, Shaq dropped 46 points and 17 rebounds in Game 1 before going for 23 points and 19 rebounds in a blowout win in Game 2. Some would say it was easy pickings for the Lakers from then on.

But the Sacramento Kings fought back. Vlade Divac, who the Lakers traded for to get Kobe back in 1996, held his own against O'Neal. Shaq struggled in Games 3 and 4 in Sacramento as the Kings came out with wins in those two games. Coming into the do-or-die Game 5, Shaq was nervous but confident he could pull off a win for his team. That he did. Shaquille O'Neal finished the Game 5 win with 32 points and 18 rebounds to proceed to the next round.

The Los Angeles Lakers breezed through the Phoenix Suns in five games in the second round of the playoffs. It was also a playoff reunion between Shaquille O'Neal and former teammate Penny Hardaway, who was already a shell of his former self that time because of injuries that robbed him of his explosiveness. O'Neal averaged 30 points and 16 rebounds that series. He started the series off scoring at least 30 points in the first three games. That included a 30-point, 20-rebound performance in Game 2.

The Lakers' real test in the playoffs came during the Western Conference Finals when they met a gritty and physical Portland Trailblazer team that had two towering big men in Arvydas Sabonis and Rasheed Wallace, who could both give Shaq a beating inside the paint. While O'Neal started the series with 41 points in Game 1, the rest of it was brutal and physical.

The Lakers managed to get a 3-1 lead after Game 4. However, the Blazers kept fighting and would tie the series up and force Game 7. The final game of the series was a defensive bout. Portland kept bodies on Shaq the entire game to keep him off the boards and limited him to just nine shots that night. They even led the game by 17 points coming into the fourth quarter.

But Kobe Bryant, together with the role players, led a furious rally to get the Lakers back into the game. Heading into the final seconds of the game, the Lakers were up four points, but Portland kept fighting. It was then and there when the most iconic play of the Shaq-Kobe Lakers era happened.

Bryant brought the ball up from the top of the key and crossed Scottie Pippen, one of the greatest perimeter defenders of all time. Running towards the paint, Kobe notices that the defense helped out on him leaving O'Neal open in the paint. In a split second, Kobe Bryant lobbed the ball up to Shaq, who finished the alley-oop play with an emphatic dunk and with a look of celebration on his face. That basket was the most important one of the five that O'Neal made the entire night. It was also the nail in the coffin for the Blazers, who could not prevent the Lakers from storming into the Finals.

That win against the Portland Trailblazers brought Shaquille O'Neal to his second NBA championship series in a span of six seasons. The last time he made the Finals was in 1995 against the Rockets. However, he was still young and too inexperienced to defend the best center, Hakeem Olajuwon, back then. O'Neal would lose in four games. But in 2000, he was the league's best player leading the league's best team. There was no stopping him from getting the crown that rightfully belonged to him.

After that tough series against the Blazers, O'Neal would find that the defensive looks he was getting against the Indiana Pacers in the Finals were easier. The Pacers opted not to double-team him. That was the biggest mistake they made. O'Neal was slamming balls down and was eating his man up in the middle to score 43 points together with the 19 rebounds he had. And in Game 2, the same thing happened. He had 40 points and 24 rebounds to give the Lakers a 2-0 lead.

But the unfortunate happened in Game 2. It was an event that nearly cost the O'Neal his first NBA title. Kobe Bryant went up for a shot. While he was in mid-air, his defender Jalen Rose seemingly slipped a foot on Bryant's landing spot. That incident sprained Bryant's ankle, and he would miss the entire game as well as Game 3. Rose would later admit that he did it on purpose.[ix]

While back then, Bryant was considered O'Neal's Robin to his Batman, Kobe's importance to the team was highlighted when the Pacers beat the Lakers in Game 3 though Shaq had another dominant night. As good as O'Neal was, he could not do it all alone. That was evident in Game 4 when the Lakers got back on track when Bryant returned. O'Neal finished the game with 36 points and 21 rebounds in overtime but fouled out of the match and was unable to lead his team to the finish. It was Kobe, with his 28 points, who led the Lakers during the extra period.

The Pacers would fight hard in Game 5 to win by 33 points against a Laker team that was seemingly gassed and out of answers. But that was all that Indiana could muster up. Back in Los Angeles for Game 6, both Shaq and Kobe were in full force to lead the Lakers to a tightly contested finish and to make sure that the Larry O'Brien trophy makes its debut in the newly opened Staples Center.

At the end of the series, O'Neal found himself hugging Bryant out on the floor and telling each other that they did it. Shaq was then sharing hugs with his family and friends as well as celebrities that began to adore what he has brought back to Los Angeles. As the night was nearing its end, Shaquille O'Neal was named the Finals MVP. After all, he did only average 38 points and nearly 17 rebounds the entire series.

Back-to-Back Champion

Being champions meant that there was a huge target on their back. Everyone was out to get the Lakers during the regular season. And when there was a big target on the back of the champions, the leader of the team had to take the brunt of those shots. The entire season, every team focused on getting Shaq out of his rhythm by constantly fouling the big man and getting physical with him. The result was a career high 13 free throw attempts per game for O'Neal. Hack-a-Shaq was in full effect that season as teams were trying to stop the defending champions.

While Shaq and the Lakers were still the favorites to win it all that season, Superman realized that the only thing that could stop him was kryptonite. Kryptonite came in the form of his teammate Kobe Bryant. It was that season when Bryant, being a champion, thought that it was already his time to shine and take the team over.[iii] He had the talent to do it. He was already arguably the best perimeter player in the league that time. But he was still teammates with the MVP and the most dominant player in the league. Shaq was still in his prime and was still putting up monster numbers.

With Kobe Bryant trying to take the team over, shooting more shots than O'Neal, and playing outside the triangle, the Lakers started the season 23-11 and did not look like the champions that they were the season ago. What was even worse was that they lost starting point guard Derek Fisher to injuries that season. Contract disputes also caused Glen Rice to be traded. Luckily, it was for Horace Grant, a master of the triangle and one of Shaq's closest teammates back in Orlando.

To his account, Shaq recalls that the Lakers began to win more games when Bryant was out with injuries for about nine games. LA would win eight of those nine games, and that was when Kobe realized that ball movement was their secret to success. Nevertheless, he still shot three more attempts on average than Shaquille O'Neal did that season.

The Lakers would finish the season with 56 wins, an 11-win drop from the previous season. Los Angeles would secure the second seed in the West while the Spurs won the first seed. O'Neal averaged 28.7 points, 12.7 rebounds, 3.7 assists, and 2.8 blocks that season. He would finish third behind Allen Iverson and Tim Duncan for the MVP voting.

Though it seemed as if the Los Angeles Lakers saw a decline that season, it was a different case come playoff time. Shaq and Kobe found harmony and were both in playoff mode. The two alpha males suddenly coexisted and started destroying the opposition with relative ease compared to the tough road they had to the Finals just a year ago.

The road to a repeat started with the Portland Trailblazers in front of the Lakers. But it seemed as if it did not matter how hard they fought the Blazers just a season ago because they completely outclassed Portland in that series. The Lakers defeated the Blazers in three easy games having won each one by double digits. Shaq averaged 28 points and 16 rebounds in that series.

Then in the second round, the Los Angeles Lakers met their rivals the Sacramento Kings, a team that O'Neal himself never had the guts to stomach. He hated the Kings, who he started calling the Queens back then.[iii] It was the same story for the Lakers in that series. They demolished Sacramento soundly in four games on their way to another Western Conference Finals appearance. O'Neal averaged 33.3 points, 17.3 rebounds, and 3.3 blocks in that series. He started Games 1 and 2 scoring 44 and 43 respectively.

While everyone knew that facing the San Antonio Spurs in the Conference Finals would be tough, Shaq admitted that he loved the idea of facing Tim Duncan. Duncan was injured in their series back in 2000. O'Neal loved the prospect of having the chance to beat Timmy, who he thought was the only big man in the league that could be mentioned in the same sentence as him at that time.[iii]

Game 1 in San Antonio was an easy double-digit win for the Los Angeles Lakers. But Game 2 almost went to the side of the Spurs. O'Neal had no answer for Tim Duncan. With that, the Lakers countered with their most aggressive scorer in Kobe Bryant, who Shaq acknowledged as an idol after bringing the Lakers back to the game and helping them beat a rival team. After that, the Lakers dominated both Games 3 and 4 by winning them by 39 and 29 points respectively. It was another clean sweep for LA.

Coming into the 2001 NBA Finals, the Los Angeles Lakers were then regarded as the best playoff team of all time. They were undefeated in the 11 games they played up to that point, and both of the Lakers' superstars were balling at the right time. Shaq and Kobe were both averaging about 30 points a game during the playoffs, and nobody could stop the duo from wreaking havoc in what was thought to be a competitive Western Conference. Matched up against the Philadelphia 76ers, who did not have the same firepower as the Western teams, the Lakers were once again favorites to sweep the title series.

But the unthinkable happened. The Sixers, led by MVP Allen Iverson, fought the Lakers hard to an overtime game. Iverson capped that upset off by stepping over his defender Ty Lue, who got knocked off his feet after the MVP made a nifty move to score a basket. It was a sweet fairy-tale win for Philadelphia, who everyone wrote off coming into that series. But fiction yielded to reality.

After Game 1, Shaq and Kobe went right back to work to take all of the next four games soundly and to win their second NBA title as a duo. What Shaq thought was memorable was how he destroyed Dikembe Mutombo, who was the reigning Defensive Player of the Year that time. Everyone thought that the towering 7'2" shot-blocking giant Mutombo could beat Shaq. But O'Neal used all of his heft and muscle to negate Mutombo's length and also used his mobility and footwork to get past the slower big man. At the end of it all, O'Neal averaged 33 points, 16 rebounds, 5 assists, and 3.4 blocks against the man people thought could stop him. Shaq would win his second Finals MVP.

Completing the Three-Peat

During the offseason after the Lakers won back-to-back titles, Shaquille O'Neal underwent surgery to fix an arthritic big toe. Shaq had the option of having a more invasive and serious surgery to repair the toe but chose not to because the recovery time would have kept him out of a lot of the Los Angeles Lakers' early season games.[iii] But O'Neal would later think that choosing the easier road might not have been the best decision.

Shaquille O'Neal would lead the Lakers to win 16 of their first 17 games of the season. Despite the terrific start to the season, it was clear that O'Neal's toe was bothering him. In his own words, the toe was "killing him" and was preventing him from pushing off with that foot. The numbers showed how much he was struggling. In those first 17 games, he was averaging 26 points and 11 rebounds. And while he was still shooting over 50% from the floor, there were a lot of those 17 games where Shaq was shooting subpar from the field. Despite that, there was still a game where he had 46 points on nearly 80% shooting. That was on December 5 against the Dallas Mavericks.

Shaq would miss a few games in December but would come back early in January 2002. However, he had a slow start to his comeback. He failed to register double-doubles in four of his first ten games since coming back. He averaged 26 points and only nine rebounds during those ten games. The Lakers did not fare well either as they went on to lose half of those games.

After making the All-Star Game yet again as a starter for a total of already ten times in his career, Shaquille O'Neal found traction later on in the season when he posted three 40-point games in a span of only five games. During that run, he averaged 31 points and 11 rebounds while making a ridiculous 65% of his shots from the field. And while O'Neal would admit that he was still feeling pain from his injury, he still powered throughout the season to give the third seed in the West after the Sacramento Kings, who were gaining traction, won the division and the top spot in the conference.

At the end of that season, Shaquille O'Neal averaged 27.2 points, 10.7 rebounds, and three assists while his minutes decreased to 36 a night due to injuries and the wear and tear his body has taken the last ten seasons. Despite that, he was still the league's most efficient shot maker and was voted to the All-NBA First Team for the fourth time in his career.

In the first round of the playoffs, the Lakers would again quickly sweep the Portland Trailblazers in three games but not in the same dominant fashion as they did a year ago. Up next were the San Antonio Spurs team that featured Tim Duncan, who had just won the MVP that season. O'Neal was seemingly struggling against the Spurs defense in that series. He shot below 50% in three of the five games they played. However, they still defeated San Antonio in five games thanks in large part to how Kobe and the rest of the team stepped up. Shaq averaged only 21 points and 12 rebounds against the Spurs in that series.

The Los Angeles Lakers' toughest test in their entire dynasty came in the 2002 Western Conference Finals against the Sacramento Kings. It was one of the most physical and hardest fought playoff series of all time. The defense was physical, and the calls were considered controversial. The series would have even gone the way of the Kings had Robert Horry not made a buzzer-beating three-pointer in Game 4 to win the game for the Lakers. Bryant took the last shot in that game but missed. O'Neal tried to put it back but also missed. The ball was then tapped out to Robert Horry at the top of the key, and he hit a cold-blooded shot give the Lakers the win.

Game 7 of that series remains one of the most controversial games in the history of the playoffs. In that overtime classic, conspiracy theorists would say that the officials were calling fouls in favor of the Lakers considering that they think they saw calls that were questionable at best especially when they were fouling O'Neal. But Shaq, true to his word that he would make his free throws when they counted the most, made 11 of his 15 foul line shots to give the Lakers that overtime win. Controversy aside, the Lakers' stars won that game when they were needed to.

Facing a Jason Kidd-led New Jersey Nets, who had a hard time coming out of the East that season, the Lakers were, of course, the title favorites once again. Nobody in the undersized Nets frontline could stop O'Neal, who was not even at this bests form the entire playoffs. Shaq demolished the Nets in four games en route to his third NBA title and third Finals MVP trophy. He averaged 36 points and 12 rebounds the entire series.

After that third championship, that Laker team became only the fifth team to three-peat. The first team to do it was the Minneapolis Lakers back in the 50's. The Boston Celtics, who dominated the 60's, followed. Then the Chicago Bulls did it twice in the 90's. Adding credence to his name as one of the greatest coaches in league history, Phil Jackson won his third three-peat. He was the very same coach that led the Bulls to those six titles in the 90's.

More importantly, that third title also solidified that Lakers team's place in history as one of the greatest squads in the history of the sport. They are consistently ranked amongst some of the greatest teams such as the 1996 Bulls, the 2015-17 Warriors, and the Showtime Lakers back in the 90's. And when one asks who was leading that team, the first name that would come to mind is rarely Phil Jackson or Kobe Bryant. More often than not, Shaquille O'Neal gets the nod for putting that Los Angeles Lakers dynasty on the map of the NBA's greatest teams.

Injury Season, Front Office Friction, End of the Laker Title Run

After Shaquille O'Neal had wrapped off that three-peat, the first thing that came to his mind was to get that big toe patched up. He was given three options: the first was the same procedure he had a year ago, the second would keep him out for three months, and the third would have kept him for about six months, but was a more guaranteed approach.

Shaq took a while with his decision. He was still negotiating a contract extension with the Lakers, but the front office was stalling because they were putting their marbles on Kobe Bryant as the future of the franchise. Because of that, O'Neal decided to take the surgery that would take three months for him to recover out of fear that being absent for an extended period might hurt his contract negotiations with the Lakers. When asked why he took his time before taking surgery, he said what he now considers one of the worst things he could have said: "I got hurt on company time, so I'll heal on company time."

O'Neal would miss the first 12 games of the season because of his injury. He came back on November 11, 2003, but the Lakers were still struggling as well as he did. They went on to lose 11 of their first 30 games and did not seem like the title winners that they were the past three seasons. O'Neal himself also did not look like his old dominant self though he was still putting up great numbers for the Lakers.

One of the highlights in the history of basketball that season was the first meeting between Shaquille O'Neal and then Chinese rookie Yao Ming, who stood 7'6" and weighed over 300 pounds. Shaq has had the opportunity to face centers that towered over him but were too skinny and slow to keep up with him. Yao was different. He not only was a lot taller than O'Neal but was also big and mobile for his size.

In one of the most viewed sports event in the history of the NBA, Shaq dominated the rookie. He finished with 31 points and 13 rebounds while Yao Ming had 10 points and ten rebounds. Nevertheless, the Yao and the Houston Rockets came out with the win that night. And that was not the only time when Yao beat Shaq. The abundance of Chinese fans voting for Yao led to the 7'6" giant beating O'Neal out for the starting center spot in the All-Star Game in 2003. That was only the second time in Shaq's career at that point where he would not start the midseason classic.

O'Neal, though having recovered from his surgery, was still feeling the effects of the injury on his big toe. As such, he was not as explosive or mobile as he would have wanted to be the entire season. Despite that, he helped the Lakers win 50 games that season to make the playoffs as the fifth seed in the Western Conference. However, it seemed as if the Lakers were not title favorites that season.

Shaquille O'Neal averaged 27.5 points and 11.1 rebounds in his 11th season and played only 67 games. For the first time in his career, O'Neal was not the leading scorer of his team. Kobe Bryant was averaging 30 points that season and was the league's leader in total points scored that season and was second in points per game to Tracy McGrady. At that point, it was quickly becoming evident that the Lakers were heading towards making Bryant the main man of the team as O'Neal was aging and physically deteriorating.

The NBA would implement a change that made all playoff series a best-of-seven, which meant that even the first round would have to be won by securing four victories. The Lakers did just that against the Minnesota Timberwolves but struggled to get there. The Wolves took a 2-1 series lead after Game 3 before the Lakers put on their championship experience to win it in six games. Playoff Mode Shaquille O'Neal averaged 28.7 points and 15 rebounds in that series.

The end of the road would come against the San Antonio Spurs. The Lakers would lose Games 1 and 2 but would come back home to tie it after Game 4. The series would have gone an entirely different way when Robert Horry had a chance to win Game 5 on a final second attempt. But he missed. The Lakers would also lose Game 6 as the Spurs became worthy successors to their championship.

Teaming Up with Malone and Payton, Shaq-Kobe Feud Erupts, Final Season in LA

During the offseason of 2003, two future Hall of Famers were free agents and were looking for a team to win their first title with. Karl Malone has been to two NBA Finals with the Utah Jazz only to lose to Jordan and the Bulls in those two battles. Gary Payton, who has built a legacy with the Seattle SuperSonics, has long been considered the best defensive point guard in league history but has seen his share of losing in the NBA Finals as well. The Lakers wanted to bring them to Los Angeles, and O'Neal helped with the recruitment process. Both Malone and Payton signed with the Lakers for sums much less than they would have made with their former teams, and they did that for a chance at their first title.

But Shaq also had his own problems while recruiting both Malone and Payton. He was asking the Lakers front office for a hefty extension with the team. But team ownership was unsure of giving O'Neal a large sum of money considering that he was aging and that his physical deterioration had led him to miss a lot of games the past three seasons.

But that was not Shaq's only problem. Tensions between himself and Kobe Bryant were also rising. In an interview, Kobe said that Shaq was all about the money but was not worth what he was asking for because of his injuries and because he was coming in every year fatter and less conditioned. He was not wrong on that though because Shaq was already weighing above 350 pounds at that point in his career.

That instantly got Shaquille O'Neal fuming with anger. He wanted to get at Kobe, but teammates intervened telling both of the players that their squabble was petty and that it was going to hurt the team's chances at a championship that season. The two would eventually hug it out and agree on a truce, but the feud was not over. And for Shaq, there still was no extension for him at the table.[iii]

The addition of both Malone and Payton gave the Lakers extra weapons on the offensive end, though those players were already past their prime. They would help alleviate a lot of the defensive pressure and offensive burden away from O'Neal, who was still nursing his injured toe. The Lakers would win 20 of their first 24 games that season and were becoming championship contenders again.

But Kobe, who was facing problems with a court case at that time, was trying to use the basketball court as an escape from all the stress that wore him down. He tried to be the alpha male in a team with three other fellow future Hall of Famers. Shaq was not happy with Bryant taking ill-advised and low percentage shots. Despite the truce between the two, the relationship had already gone down to its lowest. The two players would relay their messages across through reporters, who were more than willing to make stories out of the feud. It just came to a point where both Shaq and Kobe were seemingly going in directions that would not have benefited the team or their careers.

By February of 2004, Shaquille O'Neal had gotten the Lakers' final offer for his contract extension. Originally, Shaq wanted a three-year deal worth $30 million a year. Instead, the Lakers offered him a two-year contract that would pay him $20 million a season. O'Neal did not like the idea of taking a pay cut after all that he had done for the team since 1996.ⁱⁱⁱ It also seemed as if the front office was starting to favor the younger Kobe Bryant at that point.

The Lakers would take a huge hit again when Karl Malone got injured mid-season. He would return by playoff time but was not the same player he was before the injury. Luckily for the LA Lakers, O'Neal and Bryant never had another major issue in the middle of the season. They kept things professional and tried to win every game that they could. The Lakers would win 14 of their final 17 games to secure a top seed in the postseason.

At the end of the regular season, Shaquille O'Neal averaged the lowest number of points he had in his career at that point. He was norming 21.5 points together with 11.5 rebounds, 2.9 assists, and 2.5 blocks. But it did not matter so much because the Lakers won 56 games to stay competitive in the Western Conference. All that O'Neal had in his mind was to win his fourth ring.

The opening round of the playoffs was tough for Shaq because he had to go up against Yao Ming inside the paint. His numbers proved how tough of a battle it was for him. He averaged only 16.2 points and 11.2 rebounds in those five games. But the Lakers had too much firepower. They defeated the Rockets 4-1 and were heading into a clash with the Spurs, who beat them a season ago.

Somehow, the higher seeded Spurs looked like they were on their way to beating the Lakers again after taking both Games 1 and 2 by 10 points each. But in Los Angeles for Game 3, Shaq only missed two of his 13 shots to score 28 points while also grabbing 15 rebounds to give the Lakers a huge win. They would also take Game 4 to tie the series up. Then a miracle happened in Game 5.

Down a single point with only 0.4 seconds left on the clock, the Lakers had the ball and were looking to inbound it. The Lakers had four Hall of Famers to get the ball to and make that final shot. However, the only open man was Derek Fisher, who got the ball and quickly turned around to get off a shot as fast as he could. As soon as the final buzzer sounded, the ball found its way through the bottom, and the Lakers won. And with 17 points and 19 rebounds in Game 6, Shaq helped LA defeat the Spurs to advance to the West Finals, where they defeated the Minnesota Timberwolves in six games.

Coming into the NBA Finals against a gritty and physical Detroit Pistons team, everybody in the world knew that the Lakers were the favorite. They had Shaq and Kobe, arguably the most dominant duo in league history. They also had two future Hall of Famers both hungry for their first title win. On paper, the Los Angeles Lakers were the superior team. However, they simply forgot to play like it.

Though Shaquille O'Neal was getting his numbers, was pounded and doubled by the Pistons' big men down in the paint. Meanwhile, both Malone and Payton were getting neutralized. Kobe tried to play hero ball, but the Pistons would swarm at him whenever he attempted to get the Lakers back in the series. As a result, a fourth ring between Shaq and Kobe could not materialize. The Pistons beat them in five games and O'Neal had played his final game for Los Angeles on June 15, 2004.

During the offseason following that loss to the Pistons, the Los Angeles Lakers announced that they would be extending Kobe Bryant's contract but were unsure of Shaq's future with the team. They even considered trading him. That was the final straw for O'Neal. It was never about the money for him; it was more about loyalty and how he was treated. What was worse was that the front office was not even willing to extend Phil Jackson, who was also having troubles with Kobe being "uncoachable."

Speaking of Phil, Shaq knew that his coach was aware of everything going on between him and Kobe. But Jackson never tried too hard at getting the two to become buddies. He never tried to make Bryant tone his aggressiveness down because he wanted the All-Star guard to keep attacking. And for Shaq, he thought that Phil was milking the two players' competitive drive. Phil Jackson knew that what drove Kobe was Shaq and what drove Shaq was Kobe. The two players tried so hard at proving themselves to one another that it was beneficial to the team at the start. But two alphas could not coexist. Phil was also aware of that but decided to take his chances anyway with what the Shaq-Kobe could give him.[iii]

With things blowing up between Shaq and Kobe and the relationship between Superman and the front office going south, a trade was the best option for the Los Angeles Lakers and their two stars. The Miami

Heat came knocking and offered an enticing package of Lamar Odom, Caron Butler, and a first round pick. The Lakers accepted it and shipped Shaq over to Miami.

It was not the most fitting end to one of the greatest dynasties in NBA history, but it had to be done. In eight seasons with the Los Angeles Lakers, Shaquille O'Neal averaged 27 points, 11.8 rebounds, and 2.5 blocks. He was the league MVP in 2000 and gave the team three straight NBA championships at the height of that dynasty. But all things had to come to an end.

Both Shaq and Kobe would have fresh starts. Bryant would, later on, win two more titles as the unquestioned leader of the Lakers and even an MVP for himself in 2008. Some of his most memorable moments also came during the post-Shaq era of the Lakers. Bryant would also go down as one of the greatest ever to play the game and the league's third all-time leading scorer. Meanwhile, Shaq also had his fair share of success down in Florida. After all, success followed O'Neal's footsteps.

First Season in Miami, Teaming Up with Dwyane Wade

Coming into his first season in Miami, Shaq forgot all about the Lakers and Kobe. Instead, he focused on a younger guard who he thought was just going to be as unique as Bryant. That young guard was Dwyane Wade. Shaq knew that Wade had talent even when he was just a rookie a season before. He was a vicious attacker that was not afraid of contact. But Shaq also knew he could not repeat the problems he had with Kobe. With that, he tried to communicate and get close to Wade as much as he could. He tried a different approach with D-Wade considering that he was a different personality compared to Kobe Bryant.[iii]

Shaq also saw a few familiar faces in that Miami Heat roster. They had his former Laker teammate Eddie Jones, who was already a veteran in the league. Shaq also became teammates with former college rival Christian Laettner, who was down to his last legs that season. The Heat would later also acquire Alonzo Mourning. Once they did, they had all three of the top three picks of the 1992 NBA Draft on their team. But among the three players, Shaq was the only one who could still actually impact a game. He was still 32 years old, after all.

O'Neal made his Miami Heat debut on November 3, 2004, against the New Jersey Nets. He had 16 points and five rebounds. His first breakout game for the Heat came against the Spurs on November 12 in only 21 minutes of play in a blowout win. He had 23 points and 21 rebounds but would end up losing to his former rivals.

One of the highlights that season for Shaquille O'Neal was on December 25 when the Heat met the Lakers in a battle between former teammates turned bitter rivals. That return game to Los Angeles went into overtime. Kobe was becoming Kobe and scored 42 points that night while trying to bring the Lakers a win. Meanwhile, O'Neal may have only had 24 points, but ended up with the win thanks to an overall team effort.

The Miami Heat coaching staff that season was judicial with how they used Shaq O'Neal, though the big man would claim that his body was often tired with trying to trim his body fat down to the desired proportions of the front office. But even with that, O'Neal was shooting his best field goal percentage that season and turned the season around for the Miami Heat.

Coming into the Miami Heat, O'Neal already understood that he was not going to be The Man. The Heat wanted D-Wade to take the leadership mantle. Shaq knew and understood that but played his role as the second option to perfection to the point that he was an MVP candidate that season. O'Neal nearly won his second MVP award, but the Phoenix Suns' Steve Nash ended up winning it narrowly. He was only seven first place votes ahead of O'Neal for that award.

At the end of the regular season, Shaquille O'Neal averaged 22.9 points, 10.4 rebounds, and 2.3 blocks. He shot a then career best 60.1% from the field to lead the NBA in that department. O'Neal also led the Heat to the top of the East standings with 59 wins during the regular season.

In the first round, Shaq and the Heat quickly swept the New Jersey Nets in four games. A hobbled O'Neal only averaged 18.3 points and 8.8 rebounds in that series considering that it was Dwyane Wade who did most of the heavy lifting. Thigh injuries would keep him out of two games against the Washington Wizards in the second round, but the Heat swept their opponents anyway.

Unfortunately for Shaq, his Pistons demons came haunting him again. The Detroit Pistons defeated them in a hard fought seven game series that was physically brutal to O'Neal, who only averaged 20.6 points and 7.6 rebounds in that series. He was getting kicked out of the paint and clobbered by opposing big men while his thigh was bothering him. A fourth title ring would have to wait for O'Neal.

Fourth Title

The Miami Heat would acquire several new veteran pieces for the 2005-06 season. The first was point guard Jason "White Chocolate" Williams, who was one of the sickest passers the league had ever seen. Then there was James Posey, who was one of the best defenders in the league. They also added former All-Stars Antoine Walker and Gary Payton, who Shaq felt like he owed a title to after they failed to win one back in 2004. With the way the Heat invested in veterans that season, it was clear that they were built to win it all.

Unfortunately, the Heat stumbled into a roadblock early on. Stan Van Gundy would start the year coaching the Miami Heat to 11 wins in their first 21 games. The disappointing start led to his departure from Miami. Replacing Van Gundy was none other than the Heat president himself Pat Riley, who already had a total of seven championship rings during his time as a player, assistant, and head coach.

At first, Shaq did not want to play for Pat Riley. Riley was known for his hard practices that lasted for hours. He liked working his players to the limit almost every day. What was worse was that Riley wanted all of his players to trim down their body fat. That was one of the reasons O'Neal was so injury-prone during his time in Miami. He felt like he was working his body so hard to lose fat that he ended every day exhausted. Moreover, losing fat meant that he lost the cushioning that helped him absorb blows inside the paint. His tired body and the physical punishment he had received over the years led to him getting injured in just the second game of the 2005-06 season.

Not all of O'Neal's fears about Riley came true. Knowing that he had a veteran and aging team with him, Pat Riley turned down the volume of his practices. He was even judicial about Shaquille O'Neal's minutes when the big man returned from injury. Shaq, who only averaged a little less than 31 minutes that game, played the lowest minutes he had for his entire career during that season.

One of the highlight games for the Heat and O'Neal was on Christmas Day when Miami hosted the Lakers for another meeting between two former teammates. Shaq would again have Kobe's number that night. He not only finished with the win but also added 18 points and 17 rebounds against his former team and the man he won three titles with a few years back.

Always known as the Superman of the league, Shaq was not happy to find out that there was another physically gifted center in Florida gaining momentum as the new Man of Steel in the NBA. That player was the Orlando Magic's Dwight Howard, who stood at about 6'11" and was at least 260 pounds of lean muscle. He was quick, strong, and athletic, but not as huge as Shaq was.

The then 20-year-old center was no match for the original Superman when they first met that season. O'Neal dominated him for 25 points and 11 rebounds in addition to a win on February 14. They met again a day later, though Shaq failed to replicate his performance despite winning the game against the Orlando Magic. It was nearly ten years from that they when O'Neal left Orlando for LA. It took a decade for the Magic to replace the franchise center that Shaq was, though Howard would not develop into a player as dominant as the original Superman.

At the end of that season, Shaq averaged 20 points and 9.2 rebounds. That was the first time in his career that he did not average a double-double considering he was playing only 30 minutes a night. Nevertheless, he shot a league-high 60% from the field and helped the Magic win 52 games during the regular season. O'Neal was beginning to understand that he no longer was the franchise player that could carry a team on his back. The Heat belonged to Dwyane Wade. As legendary of a player as Shaq was, Wade was The Man in Miami. But at that age, O'Neal no longer cared. What he was focused on was winning another title and helping the young guard, who he nicknamed "The Flash," develop into one of the best stars in the league.

The playoffs started, and the Miami Heat won Games 1 and 2 against the Chicago Bulls in the first round. The Bulls fought back in Chicago to tie the series up but would end up losing the next two games. In Game 6, which was the clincher, Shaquille O'Neal finished with 30 points and 20 rebounds after underperforming in the first five games of that series.

In the second round, the New Jersey Nets gave the Heat a slight scare by taking away Game 1. But the Miami Heat roared back to take away Games 1 to 3 by double digits. Then, in Game 4, it went down the wire, but Miami held on to win the series in five games. O'Neal averaged 18.6 points and 7.2 rebounds during that series.

The Eastern Conference Finals came, and it was once again another opportunity for Shaquille O'Neal to exorcise his Detroit Pistons demons. Though he was no longer the centerpiece of the offense, he was a large factor in how the Heat were able to match the Pistons blow for blow during that series. The Miami Heat would take the series 3-1 after Game 4, but Detroit battled back in Game 5. Then, in Game 6, both O'Neal and Wade were unstoppable on their way to a win and the franchise's first NBA Finals appearance. In that clincher game, Shaq had 28 points and 16 rebounds. He missed only two of the 14 shots he took.

The 2006 NBA Finals was a meeting between two teams that have never won a trophy or even make the championship round in their respective franchise's history. It was going to be a season of firsts for either the Heat or the Dallas Mavericks that season. But it seemed like the Mavs were the ones looking to win their first title after they started the series 2-0 and won each of those two games by double digits and with O'Neal struggling.

Come Game 3, O'Neal understood that he was no longer the Finals MVP he was back during the Lakers dynasty. If there was a man that could bring the Heat back, it had to be Dwyane Wade. Shaq went over to D-Wade and told him that he reminded him of himself back in 1995 against Hakeem Olajuwon and the Houston Rockets. O'Neal thought that Wade was too respectful and nice in those first two games. If he wanted to win a title, he had to be aggressive.[iii] The Flash obliged.

D-Wade put on a show of a lifetime in the next four games thanks in large part to how O'Neal egged him on to be aggressive. He was attacking the basket, and nobody on the Dallas Mavericks' roster could stop him from doing what he wanted to do. The entire series was an ugly display of fouls and free throws. Wade made most of his foul shots while Shaq contributed by making the ones that mattered. In the end, the Miami Heat won four straight games to win the NBA title. D-Wade was named Finals MVP.

Shaquille O'Neal, who publicly promised back in 2004 that he would win a title for the city of Miami, had fulfilled what he had told the Heat fans. The Miami Heat were champions for the first time. Shaq had his fourth ring. What made that title unique for O'Neal was that he won it outside of Los Angeles and that he proved that he could win the title anywhere. Pat Riley felt the same way considering that his last six titles were won in LA. O'Neal and Riley shared a moment after that win. All that Pat Riley could tell his fellow champion was "We're back."

The Injury Season, the Beginning of the End for Shaq

Just six games into the 2006-07 season, Shaquille O'Neal would go down with yet another injury. At first, it seemed like a simple hyperextended knee, but it turned out to be worse. Shaq had torn cartilage that needed surgery. He missed a total of 35 games that season and was not the same ever since. O'Neal would return on January 24, 2007, scoring only 5 points. He struggled to get back to form after returning but would still be voted in as a starter for the Eastern All-Stars.

Shaq was not the only one bit by the injury bug. Dwyane Wade had a bad wrist all season long and would later dislocate his shoulder. He would miss a total of 31 games the entire season but was still able to put up good stats and make his way into the All-Star Team again. However, with the two Miami stars missing major time that season, the Heat would stumble to get into the playoffs. They would win only 44 games.

At the end of O'Neal's third season with the Miami Heat, he played only 40 games, which were not even half of the full 82. He averaged 17.3 points and 7.4 rebounds. What was worse was that he was quickly losing his status as a dominant presence inside the paint. Other athletic and younger big men such as Amar'e Stoudemire and Dwight Howard were quickly becoming the new Supermen of the league. But there has always been only one Superman in the history of the league. Sadly, he found out that time was his Kryptonite.

The Miami Heat would not even have a chance to defend their title that season. In the first round, they were swept out of the playoffs by a Chicago Bulls team that was not even one of the top teams in the Eastern Conference. It has been decades since a defending champion was swept out of the playoffs. The Miami Heat, because of injuries and the loss of some of their veteran guys, became a mere statistic that season.

The Final Year in Miami, Getting Traded to Phoenix

The first half of the 2007-08 season was the worst that Shaquille O'Neal has ever had as a professional athlete in his NBA career. The Miami Heat were a shell of their championship roster as several key pieces had retired or had moved on to other teams. Meanwhile, Dwyane Wade was nursing another injury that limited his capabilities out on the floor. And for Shaq, age and the pain of having to wrestle his way in the paint for nearly 15 years had already worn his body out.

On December 22, 2007, O'Neal chased after a loose ball in a game against the Utah Jazz. He hurt his hip during that incident. X-Rays and MRI showed nothing structurally wrong with him but he claimed that he was in constant pain. Pat Riley never truly bought it and thought that O'Neal was merely faking it all to get away from the mess that was the Miami Heat that season. At that time, the Heat was in the middle of what was to become a 15-game losing streak. Miami only won nine games at that point of the season.

That was the beginning of the end for Shaq in Miami. He and Pat Riley realized that what they had was over. With that, the Miami Heat thought they needed to go a different way and had to move on from the Shaq era. They traded O'Neal to the Phoenix Suns in exchange for Shawn Marion and Marcus Banks. The deal signified the end of Shaq's three and a half run with the Miami Heat. The run resulted in three All-Star appearances and a lone title in 2006.

The Phoenix Suns made the trade to acquire Shaquille O'Neal as the front office was looking to move past the run-and-gun era of the team and focus more on size. Since 2004, the Suns were always one of the top teams in the Western Conference. But they would always lose to the playoffs, specifically to the Spurs, because of their lack of size and inside presence. And as history would show, one of the few players that have been successful against the San Antonio Spurs was Shaquille O'Neal. The Suns needed his size and veteran presence, especially during the playoffs.

Shaquille O'Neal's debut with the Phoenix Suns was on February 20, 2008, against no less than the Los Angeles Lakers. Around that time, the Lakers were in the middle of their first successful season since O'Neal was traded in 2004. Kobe was also the leading MVP candidate. In that game, Shaq scored 15 points and had nine rebounds, but the Suns ended up losing to the Lakers.

It would take a while for O'Neal to adjust to the Suns' style. He was sharing the paint with a fellow big man in the form of Amar'e Stoudemire. He also was not in the best shape of his life considering that he was getting old and was battered and bruised. Despite that, he had a few good games that season. On March 22 against the Rockets, he had 23 points and 13 rebounds in a win. Nine days later, he put up 20 points and 12 boards in a win over the Denver Nuggets to show that he could still be the same dominant man he used to be.

Being in Phoenix was one of the best things that could ever happen to Shaquille O'Neal at that point in his career. The Suns have one of the best training staff in the entire NBA. They were making an old Grant Hill look like he was ten years younger. Steve Nash, who was well past the age of 30, was playing as if he was 25 years old. The team doctors would help O'Neal with his treatment.

The team doctors found out that everything wrong with Shaquille O'Neal started with his injured toe. The toe, which was not bending correctly, was causing stress all the way to O'Neal's hip. The rest of Shaq's body was trying to compensate for his toe. Because of that, there was added pressure to his hip. But the training staff helped him not by having him undergo any treatment, but by helping him strengthen his core muscles and his improve his flexibility. In a matter of time, O'Neal was looking and running fine on the court.

That season, Shaquille O'Neal averaged 13.6 points and 9.1 rebounds. He normed 14.2 points and 7.8 rebounds with the Heat while putting up a double-double of 12.9 points and 10.6 rebounds in the 28 games he played for the Phoenix Suns. The Suns made the playoffs with a 55-27 record. Unfortunately for the Suns, they ran into the Spurs in the first round. They would lose in five games despite the fact that Shaq was brought in primarily to help them against the San Antonio Spurs.

Turning Back the Clock, Second All-Star MVP

In Shaquille O'Neal's second season in Phoenix, the Suns had finally decided to do away with the run-and-gun style after Mike D'Antoni left the team due to disputes with the ownership. The Suns would hire Terry Porter, who brought in a defensive and slow-paced style that differed from the genetic makeup of the team personnel except for Shaq.

O'Neal was already 36 years old and slowing down. He was no longer the spry 300-pound seven footer that ran breaks after rebounds. He was more suited to a slow-paced style where he would set up inside the paint and dominate his defender. Porter's style, along with the excellence of the Suns training staff, helped him turn the clock back as it seemed like he was 26 years old again.

One of Shaq's fantastic performances early on was when he had 29 points and 11 rebounds in a win over the Milwaukee Bucks on November 8. Six days later, he would go for 29 points and 13 rebounds in a win over the Sacramento Kings. And on December 9, he would go for his first 30-point game by going for 35 points in a win against the Bucks.

Shaquille O'Neal continued to play like a young man again throughout the first half of the season as he would average 18 points and nine rebounds in the Suns first 41 games. At that point, the Suns were also trying to get themselves into the playoffs in the more competitive Western Conference. Because of that, O'Neal was selected by coaches to play in the All-Star Game held in Phoenix.

For the first time since 2004, Shaquille O'Neal became teammates with Kobe Bryant again albeit only in the All-Star Game. The two former one-two punch rekindled the dominance that made them three-time champions back in the day. Shaq and Kobe played pick-and-roll and give-and-go in several situations. Shaq played only 11 minutes that game but scored 17 points for the winning team. Kobe led the way with 27 points. And in the most unlikely of times, the two former teammates were named co-MVPs of the 2009 All-Star Game. At that point, it seemed as if the feud had already subsided. And as a sign of goodwill, Kobe even allowed Shaq to keep the MVP trophy and give it to the young Shareef O'Neal.[iii]

Shortly after the All-Star Game, O'Neal took a time machine and went back to his old 2000 MVP self in a game against the Toronto Raptors on February 27. He made 20 of his 25 shots to score a total of 45 points in addition to the 11 rebounds he collected in that win for the Suns. That was the 49th and final time he would score at least 40 points. Then, in his next game, which was a win against the Lakers, he scored 33 points to the delight of the Los Angeles crowd that had cheered for him for eight seasons.

At the end of the season, Shaquille O'Neal averaged 17.8 points and 8.4 rebounds. He led the league in field goal shooting again after making 60.9% of his shots. He played in 75 games, which was the most he had ever played since his MVP season back in 2000. It was all thanks to the Phoenix Suns training staff, who helped him get back to form albeit only for a single season.

Unfortunately, the Suns would only win 46 games that season. Had they played in the East, they would have made the postseason. But the West was different. The Suns also saw a midseason coaching change when the front office fired Terry Porter and replaced him with Alvin Gentry. Though Gentry helped the team get back on the winning track, it was too late for them to make the playoffs. That was the first time since his rookie season that Shaq would miss the playoffs.

The Trade to Cleveland, Teaming Up With the King

During the offseason of 2009, the Phoenix Suns ownership wanted to save some cash while the Cleveland Cavaliers were looking to add a player to their frontline to help neutralize the likes of Dwight Howard in the playoffs. Then-Suns executive Steve Kerr called Shaq to make it known to him that he might be moved. O'Neal, who was always a fan of Kerr, obliged and told the executive that he would respect any move they might make.

Shaquille O'Neal was promptly traded to the Cleveland Cavaliers in exchange for Ben Wallace, Sasha Pavlovic, and a draft pick. The moment he was traded, the only thing that O'Neal said was that he wanted to help win a ring for the King LeBron James, who was still looking for his first NBA title at that point in his career. Shaq also understood that he was no longer the dominant leader he used to be. He knew that LeBron owned that Cavs team, and accepted his role as a secondary player to the King.

By the time he arrived in Cleveland, age and deterioration had already caught up to the 37-year-old Shaquille O'Neal. He was merely a role player that started for the Cavaliers, who were leading the Eastern Conference that season. His primary purpose for the team was to stop Dwight Howard if ever they would face that team in the playoffs. The Cavs could not neutralize Howard back in the 2009 playoffs because they lacked the size to do so. They were conserving O'Neal for that purpose.

However, Shaquille O'Neal would suffer a thumb injury late in February and would miss the entire regular season. He averaged 12 points and 6.7 rebounds, which were both career lows for him. The Cavs held strong and won 61 games during the regular season to secure the top seed in the East.

Shaq made his return in time for the playoffs in the first round against the Chicago Bulls. The Cavs would quickly take that series in five games while they were conserving O'Neal's minutes. Shaq averaged only 9 points in 21 minutes of action in that series. But the Cavs' run would end in the second round against a gritty Boston Celtics. The Celtics would beat the Cleveland Cavaliers in six games as Shaq would fail in his mission to win a ring for the King.

The Move to Boston, Final Season

When the Lakers won back-to-back titles after beating the Boston Celtics in the 2010 NBA Finals, Kobe Bryant said in jest that "he had one more than Shaq," referencing that he already had five NBA championships. This prompted the Celtics ownership to hire the services of a man seeking to tie that number. They decided to bring in Shaquille O'Neal.[iii]

One of the main reasons as to why the Celtics brought in Shaq was to fill the gap in the middle left by Kendrick Perkins, who was injured against the Lakers in the 2010 NBA Finals. With Perk gone, O'Neal was more enticed to go to Boston because he could fill an important role of being the big guy inside the paint for the Celtics.

Shaq would get to play with some of his contemporaries when he joined the Celtics. He had some battles with the likes of Kevin Garnett, Paul Pierce, Ray Allen, and even Jermaine O'Neal, who was also brought in during that offseason. While playing with guys his age and people that had the same sense of humor as he did, Shaquille O'Neal had some of the best days of his career in Boston.

While O'Neal would have loved to play more games and try to win a title that season for the Celtics, injuries prevented him from doing so and from playing at a serviceable level. Shaq spent most of the season on and off the lineup and would miss a chunk of games due to an Achilles injury. He would make his return on April 3 after missing 27 games, but it was clear that he was aching and hurting.

Shaquille O'Neal averaged all-time career lows of 9.2 points and 4.8 rebounds in only 20 minutes of play. He appeared in only 37 games the entire season, but the Boston Celtics made the playoffs after winning 56 games with or without O'Neal in the lineup. But during the playoffs, Shaq missed the entire first round. He returned in the second round and played only two games against a newly formed powerhouse team of LeBron, D-Wade, and Bosh in the Miami Heat. The Celtics would lose that series as Shaq failed to a fifth title ring.

Shortly after that season, Shaq announced his retirement from the game via social media. His exact words were: "We did it. Nineteen years, baby. I wanted to thank you very much. That's why I'm telling you first. I'm about to retire. Love you. Talk to you soon." It was not the ending he had envisioned. He would have liked it to end in a parade as a champion. Instead, reality yielded to fiction. O'Neal's body could no longer handle the beating that he had been going through for 19 years. He could no longer go for another title run. And so he bid well to the game that he had dominated for nearly two decades.

With a total of 28,596 points, 13,099 rebounds, 2,732 blocks, Shaquille O'Neal retired as one of the top players in the history of the NBA. Adding four championships, three Finals MVP awards, one regular season MVP trophy, 15 All-Star appearances, and 14 All-NBA Team selections makes Shaq one of the greatest to have ever played the game and may even arguably be its most dominant center of all time.

Hall of Fame Induction

More than five years to the day when Shaquille O'Neal decided to hang his boots up permanently, he was selected to be part of a star-studded 2016 Hall of Fame class. Joining him were Allen Iverson and Yao Ming, both of whom he has had epic battles against back in the day when they were still headlining the NBA. It was his time to be forever enshrined and immortalized in the Naismith Memorial in Springfield, Massachusetts.

In his Hall of Fame speech, Shaquille O'Neal remained the same free-spirited giant he always was. He thanked all of the people that led to him making the best decisions of his life and from moving from one place to another. He thanked Bryant for the times they had and for helping him move on to Miami. He even talked about Nick Anderson's missed free throws and joked about how he, a terrible free throw shooter, should not be criticizing a bad one.

But in the same funny and jovial nature, Shaq joked that he could have practiced Rick Barry's underhanded free throw form and would have scored more points than he ever did in his career. But then again, he said that he would rather be a terrible free throw shooter that would be enshrined in the Hall of Fame than a player shooting underhanded. Of course, everything he said made the crowd laugh.[x]

Chapter 5: International Career

Shaquille O'Neal would have been a member of the greatest team ever assembled, the Dream Team, during the 1992 Olympics, but the final slot for that squad was given to Christian Laettner instead. Because of that, Shaq would make his international debut in 1994 during the FIBA World Championship. He averaged 18 points and 8.5 rebounds during that tournament and was the MVP for the gold medal winning Team USA.

In 1996, Shaq was given the opportunity to play for Dream Team II together with legends such as Charles Barkley, Grant Hill, Karl Malone, Reggie Miller, Hakeem Olajuwon, and then-teammate Penny Hardaway. He averaged 9.2 points and 5.2 rebounds to help Team USA win another gold medal. That was Shaq's final appearance in international competition.

Chapter 6: Post-Retirement Career

Shortly after retiring from the game of basketball, Shaquille O'Neal immediately became a member of Turner Network Television and would begin covering NBA games as an analyst and television personality. It was his humor and jovial personality that made him an instant hit as a member of TNT's broadcast team of the NBA.

Shaq joined Ernie Johnson, Kenny Smith, and Charles Barkley as one of the analysts of TNT's *Inside the NBA*. With him in the crew, the show became one of the best segments on television and would earn numerous Emmy awards. Shaq has a mini segment within the show. True to his personality, the segment is called *Shaqtin' a Fool*, where he features the NBA's best bloopers on a weekly basis.

Chapter 7: Personal Life

Shaquille O'Neal used to be married to Shaunie Nelson, who he had four children with. Except for Taahirah, who Shaq had in a previous relationship, O'Neal had four children with Shaunie namely Shareef, Amirah, Shaqir, and Me'arah. Both Shareef and Shaqir are athletes themselves. Shareef stands 6'9" and was a five-star recruit in high school before he committed to play for Arizona for college. Meanwhile, the younger Shaqir has guard skills that his father could only dream of.

Shaq and Shaunie would finalize a divorce in 2007. After that, O'Neal would begin dating TV celebrity, Nicole Alexander. The relationship would last for only two years as the couple would go on to live with their separate ways in 2012. He would later begin dating Laticia Rolle, who he would get engaged with in 2016.

Other than basketball, Shaquille O'Neal has involved himself in numerous off the court activities in acting, music, and reality television. Shaq's first movie was the basketball-themed *Blue Chips*, which he did together with Penny Hardaway back in 1994. In 1996, he starred in *Kazaam*, a musical comedy film. A year later, he became a superhero, but not Superman. The film *Steel* was released as O'Neal became one of the first African-Americans to portray a comic book hero on film.

Regarding music, Shaquille O'Neal was always an avid rapper and would record and compose rap music. He was active in the hip-hop scene for eight years and would release five albums. His best album was the one he released as a rookie back in 1993 entitled *Shaq Diesel*.

Shaquille O'Neal has also appeared in several television shows such as *Curb Your Enthusiasm* and *The Parkers*. When he was in Phoenix, Shaq started a reality television show called *Shaq vs.*, where he would challenge professional athletes in their sport. He has also appeared in several of both WCW's and WWE's events and even started feuding with The Big Show on some occasions. He was even a surprise entrant in the "Andre the Giant Memorial Battle Royal" on Wrestlemania 32. He was able to eliminate one person in his first official WWE match.

Chapter 8: Impact and Legacy on Basketball

Standing 7'1" and weighing at about 350 pounds during his peak years, Shaquille O'Neal's physical attributes are his biggest impact on the game of basketball. O'Neal is arguably the largest player to have ever stepped foot on an NBA court. With his size and strength, nobody could match him one-on-one. His physical attributes along with his footwork and skills down in the middle has made Shaq the most dominant player in the history of the game.

Dominance is a relative word, especially in the NBA where eras differ from one another. George Mikan, who was one of the biggest players during the early days of the league, was the most dominant. Wilt Chamberlain, who was far more physically gifted than any athlete during the 60's, was unstoppable. Even today, LeBron James could be considered the most dominant player in the NBA because of his size and athleticism at the small forward position.

However, what truly makes Shaq the most dominant figure in the history of basketball is that he would have made one of the greatest players in any era. Both Mikan and Chamberlain were playing against big men far shorter and smaller than they were. Wilt would even struggle against the much smaller Bill Russell, who most centers today would tower over. But Shaq played during the golden age of the center position when some of the best and biggest seven footers converged together in one era.

Despite playing against the likes of Olajuwon, Robinson, Ewing, Yao, and Duncan, Shaquille O'Neal still emerged as the most dominant of them all. If he were a man amongst boys during the golden age of the centers, he would have made minced meat out of the smaller players back in the 60's and 70's when the rules favored the centers. And if he played in today's era dominated by guards, O'Neal would easily score over undersized centers while fitting himself well in systems that promote four players spacing the floor.

Using his dominance as his primary weapon, Shaquille O'Neal would go on to win four NBA championships, a regular season MVP, and three Finals MVP's. The big man was not only putting up huge numbers on both ends of the floor but had a large bite to his equally large bark as he would go on to become a great leader, multiple-time champion, and game-changer.

Speaking of his bark, what made Shaquille O'Neal one of the most memorable players in the history of the game was not only because he owns the paint, but also because of his personality. If there was anything in the history of the game that would be considered bigger than O'Neal, it was his character. Shaq was considered a gentle giant that loved to make jokes and laugh about any matter. He often made fun of teammates and coaches alike while making sure that everything he said was all in jest and for the pure fun of what would otherwise be a serious sport.

It was O'Neal's larger than life personality that took him from superstar status to worldwide megastar. He would consistently appear in television shows, commercial ads, movies, promotions, and any other media outlet. He was often the talk of the town and the story of the night not only because of his highlight reel dunks but also because of some of antics and shenanigans off the court.

His tendency to make fun of things in a verbal sense led him to make several "Shaq-isms" throughout his career. Shaq-ism is how O'Neal tends to add his name to certain topics or things to make them more attuned to his person. It also includes some of his best catchphrases and jokes such as "Tragic Bronson," in reference to a Magic Johnson impersonation gone wrong, or "Barbecue Chicken," which is a phrase he uses to make reference to easy pickings. Shaq-ism is also how he coined several of his nicknames such as "The Big Cactus" when he moved to Phoenix or "The Big Aristotle" when he began to quote ancient Greek philosopher Aristotle.

But it was often Shaquille O'Neal's off court shenanigans and issues that got the best of him. During his time in the NBA, he was known for locker room dramas and feuds with teammates, coaches, and team ownership. The first overblown issue he has ever had was with Penny Hardaway back in Orlando. It was a matter between two alpha males that wanted to get paid huge money befitting of their status. However, they could not see eye-to-eye in that department, and O'Neal would eventually leave Orlando.

While Shaq would later have issues with Pat Riley of the Miami Heat and the Buss family of the Los Angeles Lakers, it was his feud with Kobe Bryant that remains the most often talked about rivalries in the history of the NBA. Shaq and Kobe started out as teammates back in 1996 when the two of them first got to LA. Back then, O'Neal was an established superstar while Bryant was still a teenage rookie looking to make a name for himself.

Over time, Kobe began to become wary of his transcendent abilities as a future all-time great in the league. He was an aloof character that focused too much on basketball, on winning, and on himself to be too worried about his relationship with his teammates. He made basketball his bride and scoring was the way he showed his love for her. Meanwhile, Shaq was trying to put things together by carrying the team on his back as the Lakers' established first option.

The two players both wanted to be the star of the team and The Man that runs the squad. While Shaq argued because he had already proven himself, Bryant was too good and skillful to defer himself to O'Neal. Over time, tempers flared up and words had been spoken to the point that neither of the two players would ever see eye-to-eye again. They would split up in 2004 after two titles while everyone else in the world wondered what could have been if the two alpha males had managed to stay their egos and worked together for the entirety of their career.

But in retrospect, Shaquille O'Neal believes that what happened between him and Kobe was for the better for his career and the Lakers back then. Trying to show to Kobe that he was The Man was his driving force. Meanwhile, Kobe was becoming even better every year at a quick rate because he wanted to take over Shaq's leadership of the team.[iii] Had they not been so competitive, they might not have won three straight titles or even a single championship alone. Competition with each other drove them to become better and to become winners that changed the landscape of the NBA.

Speaking of change, Shaquille O'Neal remains one of the biggest game-changers in the history of the league. For starters, the league started to reinforce the baskets when Shaq began pulling down the rims early on in his career. The intentional fouling also found a revival in the NBA when teams began fouling Shaq deliberately to send the poor foul shooter to the line instead of letting him get easy dunks under the basket. That tactic has been named "Hack-a-Shaq." And in 2008, the league began to implement a rule regarding that tactic. When used during the last two minutes of a game, intentionally fouling a player that did not have the ball would warrant two free throws and ball possession.[xi] And because Shaq was so dominant inside the paint, formerly illegal zone defense was introduced to allow teams to cover the paint better.[xii]

Shaq himself also believes that he changed the way the game his being played in some other aspect. Today, seven footers and centers such as Joel Embiid, Karl-Anthony Towns, DeMarcus Cousins, and Kristaps Porzingis prefer stepping out of the paint to shoot jumpers all over the perimeter or even outside the three-point line. The post-up center has become a rare commodity in the league as the NBA has begun trending in a different direction.

O'Neal believes this has become such because, during his time, kids saw how much punishment he was giving and how much beating he was taking inside the paint that they began to fear venturing in the middle to wrestle for points under the basket. As he would say, players are a product of their environment. Shaq was a product of watching centers such as Olajuwon, Malone, and Ewing battling inside the paint, and decided he should do the same. But when younger players see that they did not want to take the punishment of staying inside the middle, they would resort to shooting jumpers.[xiii] That is how and why O'Neal believes he has changed the way centers play today.

Though centers play differently today, Shaq was still able to inspire a handful of centers and big men to play strong down at the post just like he did. One of the most prominent of those big men is Dwight Howard, who was often being compared to Shaq when he was at his peak to the point that they were giving him the Superman nickname.

Then there was also Andrew Bynum, who dominated the post with his size and length on his way to two championships for the Lakers though injuries would force him to leave the sport early. Andre Drummond, who is one of the biggest players in today's NBA, uses his size and athleticism well to get easy dunks inside the paint much like how Shaq used to do. Players such as Brook Lopez and Jahlil Okafor also live down at the low post though they would occasionally drift outside to shoot jumpers.

When it comes right down to it, the way Shaquille O'Neal has impacted and changed the game while leaving a lasting legacy to the sport of basketball makes him one of the biggest players the league has ever seen in both the literary and figurative senses. He is a once-in-a-lifetime kind of player that could not be duplicated. There may come a day when a player as big and as skillful as he is would dominate the game just the same or even more so than he did. But no other player can ever replicate the way he added life and joy to the game of basketball with his personality, antics, shenanigans, and pop-culture contributions.

And whether you call him Superman, Diesel, Big Aristotle, Big Cactus, the Real Deal, the Big Shamrock, Dr. O'Neal, or Shaqovic, the name Shaquille O'Neal will forever be one of the most prominent names in the history of the sport. He dominated the game not just on the floor, but outside of the court as well. He is enshrined in the Hall of Fame, after all.

Final Word/About the Author

I was born and raised in Norwalk, Connecticut. Growing up, I could often be found spending many nights watching basketball, soccer, and football matches with my father in the family living room. I love sports and everything that sports can embody. I believe that sports are one of most genuine forms of competition, heart, and determination. I write my works to learn more about influential athletes in the hopes that from my writing, you the reader can walk away inspired to put in an equal if not greater amount of hard work and perseverance to pursue your goals. If you enjoyed *Shaquille O'Neal: The Inspiring Story of One of Basketball's Greatest Centers,* please leave a review! Also, you can read more of my works on *Roger Federer, Novak Djokovic, Andrew Luck, Rob Gronkowski, Brett Favre, Calvin Johnson, Drew Brees, J.J. Watt, Colin Kaepernick, Aaron Rodgers, Peyton Manning, Tom Brady, Russell Wilson, Michael Jordan, LeBron James, Kyrie Irving, Klay Thompson, Stephen Curry, Kevin Durant, Russell Westbrook, Anthony Davis, Chris Paul, Blake Griffin, Kobe Bryant, Joakim Noah, Scottie Pippen, Carmelo Anthony, Kevin Love, Grant Hill, Tracy McGrady, Vince Carter, Patrick Ewing, Karl Malone, Tony Parker, Allen Iverson, Hakeem Olajuwon, Reggie Miller, Michael Carter-Williams, John Wall, James Harden, Tim Duncan, Steve Nash, Draymond Green, Kawhi Leonard, Dwyane Wade, Ray Allen, Pau Gasol, Dirk Nowitzki, Jimmy Butler, Paul Pierce, Manu Ginobili, Pete Maravich, Larry Bird, Kyle Lowry, Jason Kidd, David Robinson, LaMarcus Aldridge, Derrick Rose, Paul*

George, Kevin Garnett, Chris Paul, Marc Gasol, Yao Ming, Al Horford, Amar'e Stoudemire, DeMar DeRozan, Isaiah Thomas, Kemba Walker and Chris Bosh in the Kindle Store. If you love basketball, check out my website at claytongeoffreys.com to join my exclusive list where I let you know about my latest books and give you lots of goodies.

Like what you read? Please leave a review!

I write because I love sharing the stories of influential athletes like Shaquille O'Neal with fantastic readers like you. My readers inspire me to write more so please do not hesitate to let me know what you thought by leaving a review! If you love books on life, basketball, or productivity, check out my website at claytongeoffreys.com to join my exclusive list where I let you know about my latest books. Aside from being the first to hear about my latest releases, you can also download a free copy of *33 Life Lessons: Success Principles, Career Advice & Habits of Successful People*. See you there!

Clayton

References

[i] Kriegel, Mark. "Shaq's Father Learns Biology the Hard Way". *Chicago Tribune*. 11 December 1994. Web

[ii] Wise, Mike. "Shaq to Biological Father: 'I Don't Hate You'". *The Undefeated*. 9 September 2015. Web

[iii] O'Neal, MacMullan (2011). *Shaq Uncut: My Story*. New York: Grand Central Publishing.

[iv] Gaines, Cork. "Shaq Admits He Was Angry When The Dream Team Picked Christian Laettner Over Him". *Business Insider*. 21 June 2012. Web

[v] MacMullan, Jackie. "Drafting Shaq: How the Magic Feared They'd Lost Him". *ESPN*. 8 September 2006. Web

[vi] Brown, Larry. "Shaq on Hakeem Olajuwon: He's the only player I couldn't intimidate". *Larry Brown Sports*. 22 January 2013. Web

[vii] Infantino, RJ. "Horace Grant: "Egos" Destroyed Shaquille O'Neal/Penny Hardaway Relationship for the Orlando Magic". *Fan Sided*. 2 March 2014. Web

[viii] Wong, Alex. "A Chat with Shaq and Penny Hardaway About the '90s Magic". *GQ*. 14 April 2016. Web

[ix] Tredinnick, Andrew. "Jalen Rose Intentionally Injured Kobe Bryant In The 2000 NBA Finals". *Business Insider*. 19 September 2012. Web

[x] Howard-Cooper, Scott. "Shaq, Iverson, Yao Make For Epic Hall of Fame Ceremony". *NBA.com*. 10 September 2016. Web

[xi] Martinez, Jose. "10 Athletes Who Forced Sports Leagues to Change Their Rules". *Complex*. 8 March 2014. Web

[xii] Greg. "NBA Players That Caused Rule Changes". *Sportige*. 18 March 2013. Web

[xiii] Hancox, Kyle. "Shaquille O'Neal Thinks His Style Of Play Changed The NBA". *Give Me Sport*. 2016. Web